I0825097

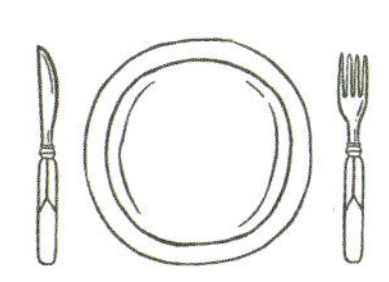

To

____

From

____

Date

____

Gather Together

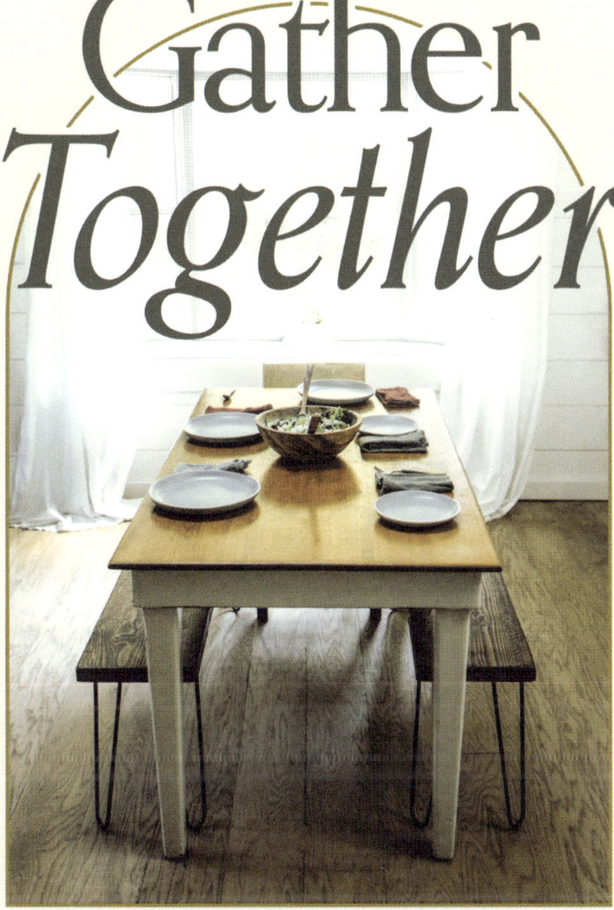

90 DEVOTIONS FOR YOUR DINNER TABLE

DaySpring
LIVE YOUR FAITH

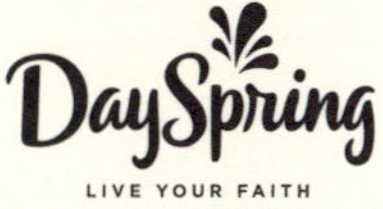

First Edition, February 2023

Published by:

DaySpring

21154 Highway 16 East
Siloam Springs, AR 72761
dayspring.com

Written by: Christy Phillippe
Cover Design by: Becca Barnett

Printed in Vietnam
Prime: J9670
ISBN: 978-1-64870-947-0

Contents

Give Him Your Worries

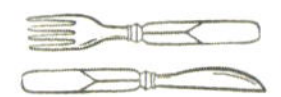

Give all your worries and cares to God, for He cares about you.

I PETER 5:7 NLT

Worry is a common emotion for all of us, young and old, boy or girl, mom or dad. We all have things that can bring anxiety each day. *Will I make a passing grade on my spelling test? What if my boss doesn't like my presentation? Will my friends think I'm cool with my new haircut? What if I can't pay the bills this month?*

Focusing on things that can go wrong—rather than relying on the God who cares for you—will always bring you down. It's still important to do your best when you can. (Study for that spelling test! Create a budget and stick to it!) But Jesus tells us that by worrying, we can't add even an hour to our lives (Matthew 6:27). In other words, worry and anxiety accomplish nothing. They won't solve the problem. They won't make things better. In fact, they probably just make things worse by wearing you out and preventing you from focusing on a solution.

If your day has been filled with the worries and cares of your life, set them all aside and remember that God cares about you!

No matter what has happened today, no matter what you are worried about right now, you can bring it to the Lord and know that He is working it all out on your behalf. It's so wonderful to know how much He cares—about *everything* that happened to you today!

Lord,
help me to bring all my worries
and concerns to You and lay them
at Your feet. I choose to trust in
You. Thank You for being with me,
no matter what I face each day.
Amen.

DISCUSSION PROMPT:

*What is your greatest worry today?
How can you focus on God's care
for you instead?*

The Truest Friend

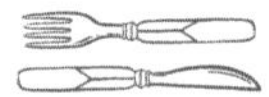

A man who has friends must himself be friendly,
but there is a friend who sticks closer than a brother.

PROVERBS 18:24 NKJV

There's nothing like a good friend, is there? Someone you can call when you've got exciting news or when something upsetting happens and you need a listening ear. Someone to go out and have fun with or someone to just hang out with on a rainy day. Someone with whom you can share your secrets, your ups and downs, the good times and the bad.

What are the qualities that make up a good friend? Honesty, loyalty, trustworthiness, for starters? How wonderful it is to have friends in our lives to share our burdens and joys. And how wonderful it is to extend those qualities of friendship to others who need to experience new friends in their lives.

Not only that, but the Bible tells us that God is our friend as well, and He is a better friend than any human being could ever be. Thank the Lord today that He is the best friend you will ever have, that He stands with you through thick and through thin.

No matter what friends you may have interacted with today, the truest Friend you will ever have stands ready to share your day. And He is closer than a brother to you. Whether you've had a terrible day or the best day ever, it's still been a day when your friend Jesus has walked by your side.

God,
thank You for the friends You
have brought into my life.
Even more, thank You for the
gift of Your friendship, which
makes even a bad day good.
Amen.

DISCUSSION PROMPT:

How has Jesus been a friend to you today?

Count Your Blessings!

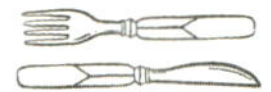

My God will meet all your needs according to the riches of his glory in Christ Jesus.

PHILIPPIANS 4:19 NIV

There is an old song that reminds us to "Count your blessings, name them one by one, Count your many blessings, see what God has done." When was the last time you did just that? When you really think about it, if you were to try to count all the blessings that you have received from the Lord, it would take you an incredibly long time—it might even be impossible!

Remembering all the good things we have in our lives is a great way to cure the symptoms of discontent and depression that can creep into our thoughts from time to time. It really is all a matter of focus: When you focus on positive things instead of the negative parts of your life, your mental state will be more positive. But it goes a bit deeper than that. When we remind ourselves of the goodness of God and all the amazing things He has already done for us, it helps us to build our trust in Him. We realize that we can count on His faithfulness to continue to bless us in the future—no matter what we might face.

In addition, reminding ourselves of God's blessings helps us to turn our eyes upward and outward. We begin to focus on God and on the people around us, and we look for ways to bless others with the gifts that we have been given. What blessings did you encounter today? No matter what today brought your way, good or bad, God has surely blessed you, and His blessings will follow you not just today, not just tomorrow, but all the days of your life!

God,
thank You for all the many
blessings You have poured into my
life. Help me never to take them–
or You, the Giver–for granted.
I will never forget all the wonderful
things You have done for me!
Help me to use all the blessings in
my life to be a blessing to others
and to point them to You.
Amen.

DISCUSSION PROMPT:

How did God bless you today?

A Circle of Kindness

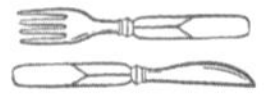

I have been a constant example of how you can help those in need by working hard. You should remember the words of the Lord Jesus: "It is more blessed to give than receive."

ACTS 20:35 NLT

Did you help someone out today? Maybe you helped out with the housework—loading the dishwasher or taking out the trash? Did you brighten someone's day by holding the door for them and sharing a smile? Perhaps you surprised someone by baking cookies for them or mowed the lawn of an elderly neighbor. When was the last time someone helped *you*?

Usually, when we are kind to another person, it makes us feel good inside. God made us that way, and often the person who gives ends up being more blessed than the one who receives the gift! It's like a wonderful circle of kindness—when we help others, we feel blessed too, and when we need a helping hand, God sends other people our way to help us.

Your day today may have been full of challenges, stresses, deadlines, and pressure to get things done. Some unexpected things may have happened, or perhaps everything went according to plan. But it's likely that somewhere along the way, someone did something kind for you—and perhaps you did something kind as well. As you reflect on God's circle of kindness, ask Him how you can be a part of it yourself in the days to come, and thank Him for all the kindness He has sent your way as well.

Jesus,
I want to be a blessing to other people just as You were when You walked upon the earth. Please help me be aware of those around me who need my help as well as those who are kind to me. Help me jump wholeheartedly into Your circle of kindness, both by showing kindness to others and by realizing the kindnesses You have shown to me.
Amen.

DISCUSSION PROMPT:

How has someone helped you recently when you needed it? What is something helpful you could do for another person?

God's Masterpiece

Lord, You have made many things; with Your wisdom You made them all. The earth is full of Your riches.

PSALM 104:24 NCV

Have you ever had the chance to see a masterpiece up close? People who have seen the *Mona Lisa* in person often marvel that it is smaller than they had imagined. No matter how amazing a man-made masterpiece is, it will never reach the level of perfection that God the Creator displayed when He made the earth and filled it with blue skies, brightly colored flowers, and an incredibly diverse array of insects, birds, and animals. But God created His highest masterpiece when He made human beings in His image.

The Bible tells us that *we ourselves* are God's masterpiece. He is perfecting you—the masterpiece that you are—through your day-to-day experiences. As you walked through your day today, He had His eyes on you, watching you with pleasure as you showed His love and beauty to those around you. And as you walk through your day tomorrow, He will be with you, perfecting everything that concerns your life.

Dear Lord,
I'm so thankful that You have made me Your masterpiece. Help me to always demonstrate to others Your love and grace, pointing them to You, the Artist who is creating a beautiful work of art in me.
Amen.

DISCUSSION PROMPT:

What works of art created by God did you observe today? Perhaps you saw a beautiful sunrise, or maybe springtime flowers or falling leaves captured your attention. Thank God for putting these reminders in your path that He loves to create beautiful things—and that includes the work He is doing inside of you!

Hoping in the Lord

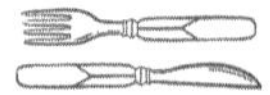

The Lord is good to those who depend on Him, to those who search for Him.

LAMENTATIONS 3:25 NLT

Have you ever trusted someone who didn't keep their promise to you? How did you feel? Disappointed, surely. Likely apprehensive about trusting that person again. When we put our hope in what other people will do for us, we are putting our hope in fallible human beings who aren't always perfect and who don't always come through. But the Bible tells us that when we put our hope in the right Person—in the Lord—He will keep all His promises to us.

If you were disappointed by another human being today—whether it was expected or a complete surprise—don't let your frustration with people carry over to God. Instead, remind yourself of how trustworthy He has been in your life, the promises He's kept, and the promises that He has made for your future. No matter how people behave, no matter what promises they keep or fall short on, you can always trust in God to keep His Word. And as you put your hope in the right place, the Lord will move in your life to fulfill His promises to you.

Dear Lord,
I'm so thankful that You are a God in whom I can trust, in whom I can place my hope and not be disappointed. When other people disappoint me, please help me to remember that they are just human beings, who don't always get things right. I choose to place my hope in You—because I know You have a wonderful future planned for me.
Amen.

DISCUSSION PROMPT:

What promises has God fulfilled in your life?

Opportunities for Joy

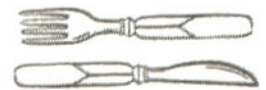

Dear brothers and sisters, when troubles of any kind come your way, consider it an opportunity for great joy.

JAMES 1:2 NLT

Let's face it. Some days seem to be filled with a lot more trouble than joyful circumstances, don't they? When you or someone you love is sick, when your family is having financial difficulties, when relationships don't go the way we wish they would, when other people disappoint us or even betray us . . . How can we find any "opportunity for joy" in that?

God looks at the situations we face much differently than we do, and He wants us to take His perspective on whatever trouble we are experiencing. If you've had health challenges or financial struggles today, you can look for joy in the situation by realizing what a loving and trustworthy God you have who cares about everything you go through. When there is conflict in a friendship, you can find joy in knowing that Jesus is a Friend who sticks closer than a brother. Whenever there is trouble, there is the opportunity to bring it to your heavenly Father in prayer, knowing that He loves you and is working all things together for

your good. No matter what troubles you have faced today, look for the joy in your situation and give thanks to God for being right there with you through it all.

Dear Lord,
no matter what I have faced today, I bring it to You and ask for Your perspective. I choose to look for opportunities for joy, even if it is just remembering that You are still in control. Thank You for guiding my life and my steps.
Amen.

DISCUSSION PROMPT:

What opportunities for joy did you experience today?

Help Wanted

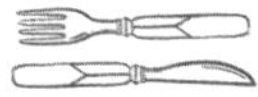

The Lord has promised that He will not leave us or desert us. This should make you feel like saying, "The Lord helps me! Why should I be afraid of what people can do to me?"

HEBREWS 13:5–6 CEV

Have you ever posted or responded to a Help Wanted ad? It can be hard for employers to find just the right candidate, but the best way to attract the help that they require is to let their need be known—either in a sign, in the newspaper, or online. There's another kind of Help Wanted notification, though, that will bring us exactly what we need—and that's prayer. When we come to God and humbly ask for His help in our lives, He responds, and He will provide us with everything that we need.

The Bible tells us over and over that God is our Helper. He is a very present help in time of need. Throughout the Old Testament, He came to His people's aid, providing them with food, water, and protection from their enemies. When Jesus came, though, He promised an even more personal help—One who lives inside of us and provides comfort, discernment, guidance, counsel, and even strength to get through the day.

The Holy Spirit is the answer to that promise, and He stands ready to be your Helper whenever you need it. Hold up your Help Wanted sign in the form of prayer whenever you need God to intervene, and the Holy Spirit—the Spirit of Christ, God Himself—will move on your behalf.

Dear Lord,
thank You for giving me help
when I need it. I'm so glad the
Holy Spirit lives inside me and
is ready to help me with
whatever comes my way.
Amen.

DISCUSSION PROMPT:

How did the Holy Spirit help you today? How can you open yourself up to more of His help tomorrow and in the days to come?

God Sees You!

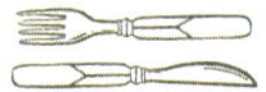

The eyes of the L*ORD* *are on the righteous,*
and his ears are attentive to their cry.

PSALM 34:15 NIV

When Sarah, Abraham's wife, was unable to have a child, the couple's desperation led them to the foolish decision of using Hagar, her handmaiden, as a surrogate for Sarah. But the circumstances were less than ideal for Hagar, and after she became pregnant, she ran away, hoping to return to her homeland of Egypt. As she was traversing the desert, the angel of the Lord appeared to her, overwhelming her with the understanding that He saw her in her predicament and cared enough to intervene. "You are a God of seeing," she called Him. "Truly," she said, "here I have seen Him who looks after me" (Genesis 16:13 ESV).

Maybe you have had the kind of day in which you think nobody saw or noticed what you were going through. Maybe you have had a day full of amazing blessings that you can't wait to share with other people. In either case, rest in the assurance that God sees you. He has His eyes on you day and night, watching over you, celebrating your victories, and sharing in your sorrows and frustrations. Not only does He watch you, but

He cares, even about the seemingly inconsequential details that concern you. There's nothing He does not see about you, and He loves you unconditionally. He's a "God of seeing"—He sees, He knows, and He cares.

Dear Lord,
sometimes it seems like no one notices or sees what I am going through. In those times, I remind myself that You are a "God of seeing," and not only do You see me, but You care immensely about the things that concern me. Thank You for Your constant care and love.
Amen.

DISCUSSION PROMPT:

What does it mean to you that God sees you? Does it cause anxiety or concern, or does it spark amazement and gratitude? Why?

Conversation Starters

Who is one of your favorite heroes, and why do they inspire you?

Would you keep a secret if you knew someone would get hurt if you did?

What is your favorite family tradition?

If you could speak another language, what would you choose?

What would you say if someone gave you a gift you already had?

How can a person become courageous?

He Knows Your Name!

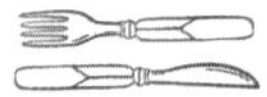

The sheep know their shepherd's voice.
He calls each of them by name and leads them.

JOHN 10:3 CEV

Four-year-old Emily was learning the Lord's Prayer by listening to it being recited at church every Sunday. One Sunday her voice could be heard over all the others as she confidently declared, "Our Father who art in heaven, I know You know my name."

As funny as this may sound, Emily wasn't wrong. God does know her name, just as He knows yours. God knows more than your name, in fact; He knows everything about you—even the number of hairs on your head! Is there anything He can't handle for you? Anything He wouldn't do for you, His beloved child? Whatever you have faced in this day, whatever you may face tomorrow, never forget that God knows you, He knows what you are going through, and He cares more than any other. The God of the universe knows your name!

Dear Lord,
how amazing it is to realize
that You, the God who created
the planets, the stars, and everything
I can see, know me by name.
And not only that but You also love
me, more than I could ever realize.
Thank You for Your steadfast care
throughout my day today—and in
all of my tomorrows.
Amen.

DISCUSSION PROMPT:

How does the knowledge that God knows your name—and everything else about you—change the way you view your circumstances today?

How Much Are You Worth?

For God so loved the world, that he gave his only Son, that whoever believes in him should not perish but have eternal life.

JOHN 3:16 ESV

What would you do if someone offered you a crisp, new one-hundred-dollar bill? You'd probably take it with gratitude. After all, you can buy a lot of things with a hundred dollars! But what if the person crumpled up the hundred-dollar bill and tossed it on the ground? You would still want it, wouldn't you? What if that person crushed it into the dirt with his foot, even spit on it? The hundred-dollar bill would still have the same value, wouldn't it?

Of course it would. The hundred-dollar bill doesn't have value because of how clean or dirty it is, because of what it has experienced, or even what it has been spent on in the past. The brand-new bill is worth the same amount as the old, crumpled-up bill, because of the value that has been placed on it.

God has placed an immense value on you. So much so that He sent His only Son, Jesus, to die in your place so that He could have a relationship with you. No matter what you have been through, no matter what you look like, no matter how you may have felt crushed into the dirt of the world, you have incredible value to God!

Dear Lord,
sometimes it's hard for me to
believe how much You value me.
I'm so thankful that You sent Jesus,
Your Son, to die for me, so that I
could have a relationship with You.
Your mercy surrounds me; Your
kindness amazes me; Your love
overwhelms me!
Amen.

DISCUSSION PROMPT:

How has God's love changed your life? How can it change your perspective on what you experienced today and what you will go through tomorrow?

The Trust of a Cat

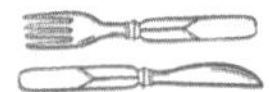

For You are my hope, Lord God,
my confidence from my youth.

PSALM 71:5 CSB

If you have a pet cat, you probably know—cats will sleep anywhere, even the most inconvenient places for their humans. So many domesticated kitties show abject terror when they are taken out of their home environments. Have you ever taken a cat to the vet before? But when they are at home with their humans, they will lie down on the floor, right in the middle of where their humans walk most frequently, and fall asleep without a care in the world. No matter that the real danger lies outside the house, not inside. No matter that if one of us were to step on the kitty, we could completely squash its head. Cats live—and sleep—in total confidence that their human companions will not hurt them (and so they typically do whatever they want!).

The next time you spot a sleeping cat—or any pet animal that relies on its human family to care for it—remember how much God cares for you. He wants you to trust Him like a sleeping cat in the walkway. As you rest in Him today, know that He is looking out for you, will meet your needs, and will keep you from all harm—today, tomorrow, and every day after that.

Dear Lord,
it's not always easy for me to
trust in You, but when I face trying
times and difficult circumstances,
help me to abandon my fears
and rest in Your care.
Amen.

DISCUSSION PROMPT:

In what areas were you willing to trust God today? In what areas did you hold back? How can you trust Him more tomorrow?

God Will Guide You

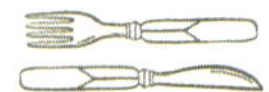

Whenever you turn to the right or to the left,
your ears will hear this command behind you:
"This is the way. Walk in it."

ISAIAH 30:21 CSB

In the autumn, under cover of darkness while the rest of the world sleeps, millions of birds are quietly taking the journey to head to warmer climates for the winter. Baltimore orioles are one such type of bird that takes the annual trip south, relying on the weather patterns and the cooler temperatures of fall to tell them to make the move. When cold fronts move in and the wind blows from the north, the birds' migration begins as they fly with the wind at their backs and the stars guiding them. The journey from Maryland all the way to the warmer climates of Mexico or Costa Rica covers hundreds of miles and can take up to two weeks. But each small bird knows exactly where it is going. God created it that way, with a GPS system built into it that guides it exactly where it needs to go, when it needs to start, and when it is time to stop.

Jesus tells us that we, God's children, are much more valuable to our heavenly Father than any bird could ever be. If He cares

enough for the birds of the sky to guide them to more comfortable and safe conditions each and every year, how much more will He give you, His beloved child, the guidance you need?

Did you seek His guidance today? Whatever your day brought you, God knows and understands—and He is ready to help guide and direct you through whatever situation you may face tomorrow as well. Listen for His voice, and He will guide your steps!

Dear Lord,
thank You for Your loving care of all Your creatures. Just as You guide the birds of the air to safety each year, I ask You to show me the direction I should take in my life. I trust You to show me the way to go, not just today but every day of my life.
Amen.

DISCUSSION PROMPT:

What decision are you facing today in which you could use God's guidance? What is He telling you to do?

God Never Changes

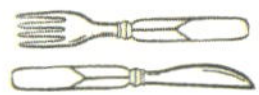

Jesus Christ is the same yesterday and today and forever.

HEBREWS 13:8 NIV

A sailor serving in the South Pacific during World War II was homesick and frightened. Everything that was familiar to him, his way of life, his daily routine, everything he knew and loved, was gone, and he found himself living a challenging life among strangers in the middle of a war in which his own personal fate was largely unknown. Standing on the deck of his ship one night, he looked up into the sky. There he was greeted with the familiar sight of the constellations he had studied back home in Ohio: the Big Dipper, the Little Dipper, Scorpio, and Gemini. Suddenly a sense of peace and reassurance came over him as he realized that the sky above him was the same sky that had always been there—just as God had never left him as well.

The Bible tells us that Jesus Christ remains the same—yesterday, today, and through all our tomorrows. Whatever you have faced today and whatever tomorrow brings for you, God's love remains steadfast. He never changes, and His plans for you remain the same—to bless you and call you His own. How wonderful is that!

Dear Lord,
remind me of Your changelessness on the days when everything seems to be changing around me. I am so thankful that in a world filled with disruption, change, and challenges, I can rely on You and Your love to always remain the same.
Amen.

DISCUSSION PROMPT:

What in the world around you reminds you of God's unchanging nature? How can you remind yourself of His trustworthiness on a daily basis?

God's Strength

Be strong in the Lord and in his mighty power.

EPHESIANS 6:10 NIV

Strength is something we all wish for but most of us need. Not just physical strength, but emotional and spiritual strength as well. When things are going well in our lives, we may feel strong, like we have things all together. But life has a way of turning that feeling upside down. Accidents happen. Diagnoses of serious illness can rattle us. The betrayal of a friend or the loss of a job can leave us feeling weaker than we ever expected to feel. Let's face it, when we rely on our own strength, we will eventually feel woefully inadequate. No matter how much we declare our own personal sense of empowerment, most of us don't have what it takes to live our lives the way we want them to be without the Lord's help.

Thankfully, we don't have to rely only on ourselves. When you come to the end of your own strength, it's time to reach out to Him for His. He has given us this incredible promise: "He gives strength to the faint and strengthens the powerless. Youths may become faint and weary, and young men stumble and fall, but those who trust in the LORD will renew their strength; they will soar on wings like eagles; they will run and not become weary, they will walk and not faint" (Isaiah 40:29–31 CSB).

When you have reached the end of yourself and all you can do is fall back into the strength of your loving heavenly Father, He will meet you there. No matter what you faced today and no matter what comes your way tomorrow, allow Him to infuse you with His strength and power today. He will never let you down!

Dear Lord,
I need Your strength, for on my own I don't always have what it takes. Help me when I am weary, and renew my strength this day.
Amen.

DISCUSSION PROMPT:

For what challenge do you most need God's strength right now?

Become a Super-Conqueror!

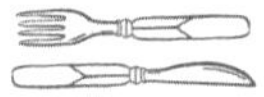

We are more than conquerors through him who loved us.

ROMANS 8:37 ESV

When Paul described believers in Jesus as "more than conquerors," he used a Greek word that literally means "super-conqueror." He meant that not only could we be conquerors of the negative circumstances in our lives, but we could super-size our conquering ability through the power of Jesus working in our lives. We can conquer the obstacles that stand in our way just as Moses raised his hands and parted the waters of the Red Sea. We can conquer the giants in our lives just as David conquered the giant Goliath who threatened the Israelite people. We can conquer the enemy's work in our lives just as God's people conquered the enemies who stood in the way of their new life in the Promised Land.

No matter what you have faced today or will face tomorrow, even if they are giant-sized problems, you can be a "super-conqueror" through Jesus, who has conquered the greatest enemy of all: sin and death. Whether hardship or pressure, heartache or distress, tragedy or disaster has entered your life, He will raise you up and help you to overcome. Become a super-conqueror and watch what happens in your life!

Dear Lord,
so many obstacles surround me
that sometimes I don't know what to
tackle first. It's hard to imagine being
a conqueror during these times, but
I'm grateful that in Your strength I
can become a super-conqueror of
whatever faces me today, tomorrow,
and the rest of my life.
Amen.

DISCUSSION PROMPT:

*What problem do you
need to conquer today?*

The Riches of His Grace

For from his fullness we have all received, grace upon grace.

JOHN 1:16 ESV

One day a young girl and her mother were walking past the house of a man who was cleaning out his garage. "Hey," the man called out. "Do you have a bike?" When the girl shook her head, he pulled a pink princess bike out of the garage. "Here, take this one—we don't need it anymore!" The mother tried to pay the man, but he refused to take any money. He was happy to just get it out of his garage, but the girl was delighted by such an unexpected and generous gift.

The gifts that God offers to us are given free of charge. There is nothing we need to do to earn them or pay for them. That's why it's called grace! He gives "grace upon grace," showering His favor into our lives. Ephesians 1 tells us that our heavenly Father loves to lavish His riches upon us. He will make "all grace abound to you . . . in all things at all times" (II Corinthians 9:8 ESV).

How did God show His grace to you today? Give Him thanks for that! And look for His grace and blessings tomorrow as well. He will delight you in unexpected and generous ways!

Dear Lord,
the extravagant riches of Your grace overwhelm me at times. Thank You for pouring Your grace and love into my life. Help me to never take Your grace for granted but always maintain a grateful heart.
Amen.

DISCUSSION PROMPT:

In what situation or relationship do you need the riches of God's grace? In what situations have you experienced His grace today?

The Real Superhero

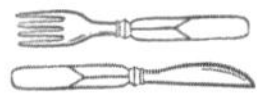

Yours, O Lord, is the greatness and the power and the glory and the victory and the majesty, for all that is in the heavens and in the earth is yours. Yours is the kingdom, O Lord, and you are exalted as head above all. Both riches and honor come from you, and you rule over all. In your hand are power and might, and in your hand it is to make great and to give strength to all.

I CHRONICLES 29:11–12 ESV

Most kids (and a lot of adults) today are enamored by the superheroes portrayed in the Marvel universe, typically ordinary people who have somehow been imbued with incredible power or skills they never expected to receive. It's all fiction, of course; we know that no human being can deflect bullets, run faster than a train, leap over the tallest building in a single bound, or even sprout wings and fly. But in some ways, we tend to think we have more power than we actually have. All it takes is one disaster, one tragedy, one phone call in the middle of the night to remind us that human beings are fragile, that life is precious, and that we aren't really in control, even of our own lives.

Thankfully, we serve the God who is fully in control, and He is the real Superhero of our lives. He has the power to do anything—think of it: *anything!* When you feel out of control, turn to the

One who controls the universe. Your heavenly Father loves you more than you can imagine, and you can trust Him to work all things out for your good when you turn to Him for help.

If God helped you today, thank Him for it! His love and constant working in our lives make Him worthy of our praise. And as He walks with you and works on your behalf tomorrow and the day after that, thank Him then as well. He's the greatest Superhero of all.

Dear Lord,
You hold all the power of the universe within Your mighty hands. When I consider the vastness of Your power and strength, I am in awe that You care about even the smallest details of my life. Help me to fully trust that You are good and You are working things out for good in my life. You did it today, and You will do it every day!
Amen.

DISCUSSION PROMPT:

In what ways did you see God's mighty power move in your life today?

Group Activity

FAMILY TREE

On a large piece of paper, draw out your family tree, going back as many generations as you can. When you have made the tree as big as possible, take turns sharing your favorite memories of the people listed on the branches.

Genius!

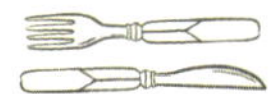

Only God has wisdom and power,
good advice and understanding.

JOB 12:13 NCV

What's your IQ? The average intelligence quotient is around 100. Albert Einstein is believed to have had an IQ of 160. If a person has an IQ of 140 or higher, they are considered a genius in the world's eyes. But does that person really have *wisdom*?

A comical illustration once showed a child genius trying to open the door to a building labeled "Society for Geniuses." Although the door had a clearly visible sign reading PUSH, the genius was pulling at the door with all his strength. The joke rings true: we have all known purported geniuses who struggled through life, lacking the necessary wisdom to make things work.

Thank goodness we don't need to rely on our own smarts—or lack thereof—to navigate our way through life. God has given us access to His own divine, supernatural, omniscient knowledge and understanding. His wisdom will grace our lives, if we only ask Him for it. As He has said, "Now if any of you lacks wisdom, he should ask God—who gives to all generously and ungrudgingly—and it will be given to him" (James 1:5 CSB).

If you needed God's wisdom today and He provided it, thank Him for it! His "good advice and understanding" is readily available, whether you needed it today or will need it tomorrow. What a wonderful God who stands ready to help! Even if you faced complicated issues or tricky situations today, He led you through, and He is willing to do the same again—all you need to do is ask.

Dear Lord,
in my own wisdom and understanding, I could never make it through life. I'm so grateful that You promise to give wisdom to anyone who asks for it, and so I ask You for Your divine guidance in my life. Help me to make not only the smart decision but also the wise one in whatever I face, today, tomorrow, and for the rest of my life.
Amen.

DISCUSSION PROMPT:

In what area of your life do you need God's wisdom and guidance today?

Happiness Can Be Yours!

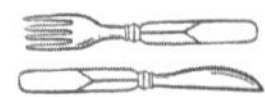

You make known to me the path of life;
in your presence there is fullness of joy;
at your right hand are pleasures forevermore.

PSALM 16:11 ESV

In America, one of our national declarations is the right to "life, liberty, and the pursuit of happiness." How happy are you on a daily basis? Are you a perpetually cheerful person, or do you constantly fight a sense of doom and gloom? All of us want to be happy, but not many people realize that that desire for joy and pleasure was given to them by God. God Himself is pure joy, and He wants you to live an abundant, joy-filled life (John 10:10; 15:11).

Often the issue in our lives is not that we are actually pursuing joy and happiness, but that we are looking for that happiness in the wrong places. God has given us good things in the world to enjoy. There is nothing wrong with a nice car, a juicy steak, beautiful clothes to wear, a big house . . . but if we are relying on those things to bring us joy, we will be disappointed. The fullness of our joy can only be found by spending time in His presence, in living to please Him in all that we do.

Did you experience His joy today? Even if it wasn't your happiest day, it is still a good day when we spend it with Jesus, who brings us fullness of joy each day of our lives.

Dear Lord,
I confess I often look for joy
and happiness in the wrong places,
in things and other people rather
than in You. As I spend time with
You today, plant the seeds of
joy within my spirit and help me
cultivate them into the blossoms
of a happy heart.
Amen.

DISCUSSION PROMPT:

What can you do to experience the joy and pleasure of God's presence in your life?

God's Extravagant *Hesed*

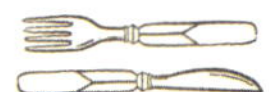

Your faithful love is higher than the heavens,
and Your faithfulness reaches to the clouds.

PSALM 108:4 CSB

God's love is absolutely enormous, but it's more than that. It's solid. It's reliable. It's a foundation you can count on. The Hebrew word *hesed* richly and powerfully describes this aspect of the love of God: its meaning includes words like *faithful, steadfast, unfailing, great, loyal, merciful,* and *kind.* We often see this word translated as "loving-kindness" in the Bible, and it depicts the most extravagant form of love that there is. This love is firmly rooted in the character of God, not anything we could ever do to deserve it. It involves a blood level of commitment, as demonstrated by Jesus' death on the cross to save us and to adopt us as God's beloved children into His family.

Aren't you thankful for this kind of love that God pours out in your life? There is no need to question His commitment to you. His love for you is steadfast, faithful, and true.

How did you experience His love today? He likely demonstrated His faithfulness in a myriad of ways. It's so good to walk each day by His side!

Dear Lord,
I stand in amazement at Your incredible, undeserved love that You so graciously pour into my life. Let me never take it for granted, but instead, help me consistently live in the light of Your grace.
Amen.

DISCUSSION PROMPT:

Which word used to describe God's hesed *most speaks to you? Why?*

How Grateful Are You?

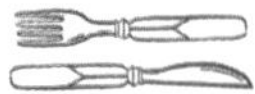

Enter His gates with thanksgiving and His courts with praise. Give thanks to Him and bless His name.

PSALM 100:4 CSB

I wonder if you know how many verses in the Bible tell us to be thankful for what we have been given or encourage us to be grateful. Maybe you would guess a hundred. Maybe you'd guess a thousand. You'd be wrong with both those answers. The Bible contains more than two thousand verses that tell us to "Praise the Lord" or "Give thanks to Him" or "Bless the Lord!" When we praise God, we focus on His character and nature, and when we give thanks to Him, we focus on all the amazing things He has done on our behalf.

Taking our eyes off of our own problems and pursuits and putting them on the Lord and what He has done does something on the inside of our hearts—it brings a different perspective, helping us to remember that no matter what goes on in our lives, we have a loving and powerful God on our side who loves to bless us with all good things. And the fact that God instructs us to do this not once, not a hundred times, but more than two thousand times—far more than He even asks us to pray or to love other people—shows its importance. What are you grateful for today?

Dear Lord,
sometimes I forget all the blessings
You have poured out on my life.
Help me to remember all the things
You have done for me, and when I
have a tough day or face challenging
circumstances, the reminder of Your
love and willingness to help will
carry me through.
Amen.

DISCUSSION PROMPT:

How many blessings can you name that God has brought into your life? How does gratitude for those blessings take your mind off your temporary problems and put it on the eternal God who pours those blessings upon His children?

How Much Does God Love You?

Great is your love, higher than the heavens; your faithfulness reaches to the skies.

PSALM 108:4 NIV

Have you seen the books that parents read to their children in an attempt to tell their sons and daughters how much they are loved? Until those children become parents themselves someday, they won't really know the overwhelming feelings of love a mom or dad has for their children, but these books try to share the message in a way the child can understand: "I love you this much," the book proclaims with illustrations of arms stretched as wide as the pages will allow. Or "I love you to the moon and back," which is as far as a child could possibly imagine.

Psalm 108 is like those children's books in the way God tries to convey how great His love is for us, His children. His love is "higher than the heavens," and it "reaches to the skies." God's love stretches past the moon into the millions of galaxies in the universe. Imagine Him saying to you today, "I love you this much—and more!"

No matter what you experienced today, remember God's message of love for you. He loves you more than you could ever know!

Dear Lord,
it's easy to forget sometimes
just how much You care for me.
I'm so thankful for Your amazing
love and for everything You do for
me each day. Remind me often
of Your love and care.
Amen.

DISCUSSION PROMPT:

The Bible says God's love is "higher than the heavens." What other metaphors could you use to describe His love?

Great Is Your Faithfulness!

Because of the Lord*'s faithful love we do not perish, for His mercies never end. They are new every morning; great is Your faithfulness.*

LAMENTATIONS 3:22–23 CSB

The beautiful words of King Solomon penned so long ago in these verses were adapted into a much-beloved poem—and later a hymn—by Thomas Chisolm in the nineteenth century. Its words remind us that no matter what we face each day, God is always with us. He is always, always, always faithful to be by our side, in good times and bad, in times of joy and happiness and in times of sorrow and doubt.

Your day today may have been ordinary, even boring. It may have been filled with challenges, problems, and trouble. It may have been one of the best days of your life. It could have been busy, humdrum, sad, or happy. It is true that you will never have complete certainty about what a day will bring. But you *can* have certainty that God will always be with you, that He is faithful and can be counted on to see you through. Great is His faithfulness—it is new every morning, every single day of your life!

Dear Lord,
in the busy days of my life and in the boring ones, in all of my ups and downs, I am so thankful that You are faithful to remain by my side. Your faithfulness is so great, Lord!
Amen.

DISCUSSION PROMPT:

How has God been faithful to you recently?

Together

You are better having a friend than to be all alone, because then you will get more enjoyment out of what you earn. If you fall, your friend can help you up. But if you fall without having a friend nearby, you are really in trouble. If you sleep alone, you won't have anyone to keep you warm on a cold night.

ECCLESIASTES 4:9–11 CEV

People need other people. God made us that way, and it's why we are born into families and why we make many friendships throughout our lives. God created us to be in relationship with one another.

Families are a very important part of our lives. They are all different and all very special. God placed each of us in our specific families for a reason. He gave us the people we live with to love us and to help us grow. Moms and dads, children and grandparents, even our pets, can help us grow together to be more like Jesus. The Bible tells us that we are better off together than we are apart, and this is so true.

How did your family help you through this day? Thank God for them, for how they made this a good day in your life, no matter what else might have happened. You might not always get along with your family members; you may have different interests, hobbies, or ideas about how things should be done. But God has given you these people to shape your life and your heart, and let's face it: we are better together than apart!

Dear Lord,
thank You for the people
You have placed in my life.
Help me never to take them for
granted but to watch for ways
I can be a blessing to them,
the way they have also blessed me.
Amen.

DISCUSSION PROMPT:

What do you love about the family in which God has placed you?

Sharing Our Emotions

Be happy with those who are happy, and weep with those who weep.

ROMANS 12:15 NLT

God created people to feel all kinds of emotions: happiness, sadness, fear and despair, joy and exhilaration. In one day, our emotions can run the gamut, depending on the circumstances that we face. Sometimes people don't want to show their feelings to others, but the Bible tells us that sharing our emotions is a good thing. When other people join with us in our laughter and our tears, they help to share our burdens and our joys. Our happiness can be multiplied, and our sorrows and burdens can be shared when we choose to "be happy with those who are happy, and weep with those who weep."

God wants us to experience all the emotions He created for the human race to feel. He wants us to feel compassion for people who seem to have no hope and show patience to those who are angry or upset. He wants us to share our joys and sorrows with each other.

No matter what kind of day you have had—a joyful day, a day full of sorrow and frustration, or a day somewhere in between—

there are people with whom you can share your feelings, and who can share their joys and frustrations with you. It's so good that God made us this way, isn't it?

Dear Lord,
thank You for all the different emotions You have placed within the people You created. Help me to laugh with those who laugh, cry with those who cry, and experience all of life with those You have placed in my life. Amen.

DISCUSSION PROMPT:

What emotions did you experience today? How can you share the laughter and joy of a good day, or the sorrow and tears of a bad day, with the people around you?

Surprise!

You have done amazing things
we did not expect. You came down,
and the mountains trembled before You.

ISAIAH 64:3 NCV

"Surprise!" Have you ever been the recipient of a wonderful surprise? Maybe it was a birthday party that you weren't expecting. Maybe someone you love showed up at your door after a long absence from your life. Or maybe you won a contest or a sweepstakes when you least expected to win. When wonderful things happen that you had no idea were coming, you can thank God for His gift of surprise!

The Bible tells us that God loves to do amazing things for us when we least expect it. It isn't possible to know what the days ahead will hold, but we can count on God to be ready for a surprise or two when we least expect it. Even if your day has been filled with challenges and obstacles, God has a way of showing up and surprising you with His love, mercy, and grace. Look for Him today—and prepare to be surprised!

Dear Lord,
thank You for being the
God of wonderful surprises!
Help me to live in expectancy
of all the good things
You have planned for my life.
Amen.

DISCUSSION PROMPT:

How has God surprised you recently?

Conversation Starters

What is your favorite thing about your life? Your least favorite thing?

How is your family different from other families?

What was your favorite family vacation and why?

What do you enjoy the most about each of your siblings (or cousins)?

How was your grandparents' childhood different from your own?

Which objects would you save first if your house caught fire?

Beautiful Music

Be filled with the Holy Spirit, singing psalms and hymns and spiritual songs among yourselves, and making music to the Lord in your hearts.

EPHESIANS 5:18–19 NLT

Music is one of very few activities that uses the entire brain. It can engage the emotional, motor, and creative areas of the brain at the same time. Music has been linked to better learning, workout performance, and emotional connections to people and experiences.

Music is used in many ways to capture emotion—in movies, in love songs played on the radio, even in advertisements to persuade consumers to buy certain products. Music taps into our souls in ways that not many other things can. That makes music a really good way to enhance our relationship with God. He tells us in His Word to sing new songs and create beautiful music for Him. As you go about your day, consider humming the tune to a praise and worship chorus or listening to music that inspires you and turns your heart to the Lord, even in the midst of your busyness and concerns. The gift of music provides so much encouragement from the Lord.

Dear Lord,
thank You so much for the gift of music. You have blessed so many people with musical talent, and I choose to join with them in raising my voice to You. Even in the middle of the cares and busyness of this world, I want to always join Your people in praising You with all of my talents as well.
Amen.

DISCUSSION PROMPT:

How has music made an impact on your life? How can praising God through music make an impact on your day-to-day life?

Get Some Rest!

Then Jesus said, "Let's go off by ourselves to a quiet place and rest awhile." He said this because there were so many people coming and going that Jesus and His apostles didn't even have time to eat.

MARK 6:31 NLT

When was the last time you went on a vacation? If you are like most people, it's been far too long! Whether your dream vacation includes warm beaches or snow-capped mountains, a cabin by the lake or exploring a foreign city, it's wonderful to get out of your daily routines at times and enjoy the world that God has created. Going on vacation allows you time to slow down, spend time with your loved ones, try new things, but above all, rest and recharge.

Even Jesus needed to get away to a quiet place at times and get some rest, and He encouraged His disciples to do the same. When we are so busy every day with different tasks, activities, and responsibilities, it can be difficult to remember that we must take time to rest—our bodies, our minds, and our spirits. No matter when your next vacation is scheduled, be sure to seek out time each day to rest in His presence. You don't need to travel to

some faraway beach or cabin in the woods to seek the refreshing presence of the Lord. He is with you here and now, and He's calling you, "Come away with Me and get some rest!"

Dear Lord,
sometimes I get so busy in my life and activities that I forget that You have called me to rest in Your presence and spiritually recharge. Remind me of this when I need to remember and woo me away from my cares and responsibilities to spend time resting with You.
Amen.

DISCUSSION PROMPT:

Describe your dream vacation. How does time spent resting with the Lord day by day compare?

Living Water

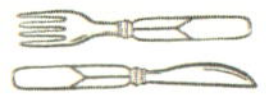

Those who drink the water I give will never be thirsty again. It becomes a fresh, bubbling spring within them, giving them eternal life.

JOHN 4:14 NLT

Did you know that more than one billion people in the world today have to travel more than fifteen minutes to get to a safe water source? About 423 million people around the world get their water from unprotected wells and springs. This means that the water they are drinking might not be safe. If you have ever had the water turned off in your home for any period of time, you understand how important it is. We need clean water for drinking, for cooking, for washing our clothes, our dishes, and our bodies.

It's so easy to take the water that we have for granted—just as it is easy to take the Living Water—Jesus—for granted. When we are thirsty, there is nothing like a nice tall glass of cold water to quench our thirst. And when we long for spiritual refreshing, there is nothing like the presence of Jesus to quench the deepest longings in our hearts.

If you are feeling dry and parched in your spirit today, allow Jesus to refresh you with His living water and remind you of the eternal life you have received through Him.

Dear Lord,
my spirit at times grows
dry and needs Your refreshing
touch. Pour Your living water
out on me today.
Amen.

DISCUSSION PROMPT:

How can you drink deeply of the living water Jesus provides today?

Choose Joy!

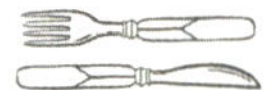

Count it all joy, my brothers, when you meet trials of various kinds, for you know that the testing of your faith produces steadfastness.

JAMES 1:2–3 ESV

During World War II, Dr. Viktor Frankl was imprisoned by the Nazis because he was a Jew. His wife, children, and parents were all killed in the Holocaust. At one point, the prison guards cut his wedding band off his finger. Frankl said to himself, "You can take away my wife and children, you can strip me of my clothes and freedom, but there is one thing no person can ever take away from me—and that is my freedom to choose how I will react to what happens to me."

No matter what the world tries to do to you, no matter what problems and challenges come your way, you have the freedom to choose—to choose how you will react, to choose to persevere rather than give up, to choose joy instead of despair. The Bible tells us to "count it all joy" when we face adversity and challenges. How can we do this? By looking to Jesus and gaining an eternal perspective on our problems. God promises to be with us in whatever we face—and because of that, we can choose joy, no matter what.

Dear Lord,
so many things come at me
in life that try to steal my joy.
I'm so thankful that You are with
me through them all and that You
prompt me to "count it all joy" when
I face these challenges. No matter
what I am faced with this day,
I know that I can count on
You to be by my side.
Amen.

DISCUSSION PROMPT:

In what area of your life do you need to choose joy today?

Keep On Running!

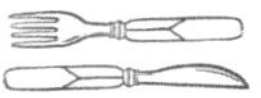

Since we are surrounded by such a great cloud of witnesses, let us throw off everything that hinders and the sin that so easily entangles. And let us run with perseverance the race marked out for us.

HEBREWS 12:1 NIV

Wilma Rudolph was the twentieth of twenty-two children. She was born prematurely, and doctors didn't expect her to survive. She did, but at a young age, she contracted double pneumonia and scarlet fever, and her left leg was paralyzed as a result of having poliovirus as an infant. At the age of nine, she removed the metal leg brace she had depended on for the past five years and began walking without it. By the age of thirteen, she had developed a rhythmic walk, which doctors said was a miracle. That same year, she decided she wanted to begin running. She entered her first race and came in last. For the next three years, she came in dead last in every race she entered. But she kept on running until the day finally came that she won a race. Eventually, the little girl who was not supposed to live, and who then was not supposed to be able to walk, would win three Olympic gold medals—because she kept on running.

If you are facing discouragement in your life today, if others have told you that your dreams just aren't possible, don't believe them, and do not quit! Keep on running, friend. Don't give up, no matter what life throws your way. With God on your side, anything is truly possible.

Dear Lord,
sometimes my race seems long,
and I am tempted to give up.
Remind me that with You on
my side, anything is possible, as
long as I keep on running. Thank
You for giving me the strength I
need to continue the course
I am running for You.
Amen.

DISCUSSION PROMPT:

In what area of life do you need encouragement to "keep on running" today?

Taking the Heat

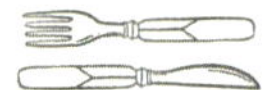

And take the helmet of salvation, and the sword of the Spirit, which is the Word of God.

EPHESIANS 6:17 NKJV

In the early 1970s, the firefighters of Fairfax County, Virginia, received new helmets as part of a budget increase in their department. The new helmets looked incredible: They were bright, shiny red, size-adjustable, made of high-impact plastic, and even scuff-resistant. There was just one problem, however: When they were worn near the heat of a fire, they melted. Of course, the new shiny helmets were ultimately useless to the firefighters; they needed helmets that could take the heat.

As a believer in Jesus, how is your "helmet of salvation" today? Is your trust in God strong enough not to melt when life gets tough? We need a faith that can take the heat of persecution, challenging situations, even outright attacks by the enemy of our souls—one that can endure the fire and protect us in the midst of the blaze. A bright and shiny faith that looks good in church or in front of other people isn't going to cut it when we find ourselves surrounded by trouble. Make sure your faith is grounded firmly in the Lord by spending time with Him in His

Word and in prayer. Then, no matter what comes your way, you will be able to stand strong, trusting in Him to see you through.

Dear Lord,
when the fires and troubles of life surround me, I'm so thankful for the faith You have put in my heart that I know will see me through. I trust You to always be with me in good times and bad. I want more than a bright and shiny faith that looks good to other people; I want my faith in You to be solid and secure.
Amen.

DISCUSSION PROMPT:

How sturdy is your "helmet of faith" today? In what ways could you make it stronger to better prepare you for the challenges of life?

Live Between Steps

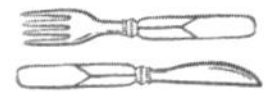

The Lord *directs the steps of the godly.*
He delights in every detail of their lives.

PSALM 37:23 NLT

A professor was invited to speak at a military base and was met at the airport by a soldier named James. As they headed toward the baggage claim area, James kept disappearing—once to help an older woman with her suitcase, once to help a struggling mother with two toddlers, and again to give someone else directions. The professor asked him, "Where did you learn to live like that?" James said, "During the war." He had served in Vietnam, where his job had been to clear minefields, and he watched friends die suddenly, one after another, before his eyes. He said, "I never knew when the next step would be my last, so I learned to live between steps."

In the many steps that each of us takes every day, it is easy to get caught up in the tasks and responsibilities we need to fulfill. The Bible tells us that our steps are ordered by the Lord—not only the obvious steps that we take by caring for our families, working at our jobs, fulfilling our responsibilities, but also what we do between those steps, the little things we do to lend a hand, offer a listening ear, or spread God's love to other people. As we live between the steps, we will experience more joy and fulfillment than we ever thought possible.

Dear Lord,
forgive me for sometimes forgetting that the greatest joys in life can often be found in the little things I do, not just in the larger responsibilities of life. Guide me always to live between my steps as I walk through my day with You by my side.
Amen.

DISCUSSION PROMPT:

How are you living between the steps in your life?

Wait on the Lord

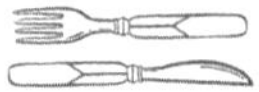

Wait on the Lord*; be of good courage, and He shall strengthen your heart; wait, I say, on the* Lord*!*

PSALM 27:14 NKJV

Some years ago, a speedboat driver who had survived a racing accident described what had happened. He said he had been at near top speeds when his boat veered slightly and hit a wave at a dangerous angle. The combined force of his speed and the size and angle of the wave sent the boat spinning crazily in the air. He was thrown from his seat and propelled deep into the water—so deep, in fact, that he had no idea which direction the surface was. He had to remain calm and wait for the buoyancy of his life vest to begin pulling him up. Once he discovered which way was up, he could swim for the surface.

Sometimes life can become confusing, and the events of our day can disorient us, immersing us so deeply into our problems that we forget which way is up. When this happens, the best thing to do is to calm ourselves before the Lord—and wait. He promises to gently tug us in the right direction as we focus on Him and gain His leading from the Holy Spirit. The key to cutting through the confusion is to recognize our dependence on His direction and trust Him to guide us in the way we should go.

Dear Lord,
there are times when the troubles and problems of my life leave me confused and disoriented. At those times, Lord, help me to wait on You and Your gentle tug to pull me in the right direction. As I am patient to listen for Your voice, help me to trust in You fully.
Amen.

DISCUSSION PROMPT:

What problems or challenges have left you disoriented lately? How might waiting on the Lord bring you the direction that you need?

Good Things Come to Those Who Wait!

For you have need of endurance,
so that when you have done the will of God
you may receive what is promised.

HEBREWS 10:36 ESV

A common sight in America's southwest desert is the century plant. It's unique, in that it thrives in rocky, mountainous, or desert terrains. It has dramatic, splayed leaves that grow up to a foot wide. The plant can reach twelve feet in diameter. But what makes the century plant unusual, as its name suggests, is its long reproductive cycle. For twenty or thirty years (not a literal century), the six-foot-tall plant stands the same height and puts out no flowers. Then, one year, quite unexpectedly and without warning, a new bud sprouts. The bud, which resembles a tree trunk–size asparagus spear, shoots into the sky at a fantastic rate of seven inches per day and reaches an eventual height of twenty to forty feet. Then it crowns itself with several clumps of yellowish blossoms that last up to three weeks.

Like the century plant, many of the most wonderful things God has for us come only after a long wait. What are you waiting for in your life today? Don't give up—God is always working in the lives of His children, even if we can't always see what He is doing. Then, one day, quite unexpectedly, the blossoms spring forth, and we receive the promise fulfilled, the hope made reality, the dream come to pass. Good things come to those who wait!

Dear Lord,
waiting is such a challenge
for me, especially when I can't
see You working in my life. Please
help me be patient to wait on You
and Your promises. I know the
fulfillment will be so worth it!
Amen.

DISCUSSION PROMPT:

What are you waiting for God to do in your life today?

Group Activity

PHOTO ALBUMS

Dust off the old baby pictures and photo albums and pass them around! It can be so much fun to look at pictures of how each member of the family has changed throughout the years. When you have finished admiring the old hairstyles and clothing choices, spend some time thanking God for His unchanging nature. Even though we may change drastically as we grow up, He will always stay the same!

God's Eraser

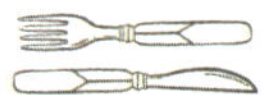

He has removed our sins as far from us as the east is from the west.

PSALM 103:12 NLT

Have you ever messed something up when you were writing? If you were fortunate enough to be writing with a pencil, you could simply erase what you had done and start again. But sometimes, even when you have erased a mistake, you can still see faint lines on the paper where the mistake was made. Or maybe you were writing with a pen or a marker and you had to figure out a different way to cover up your mistake—perhaps reword your sentence or draw a line through the words that were wrong. No matter what you did to change the mistake, even if it was erased perfectly, you still knew where the mistake was made.

As we go through our day-to-day activities, there are many opportunities to make mistakes, to miss the mark. The Bible calls it "sin." When this happens, many of us replay the mistake over and over again in our minds. We remind ourselves of what we have done and continue to feel ashamed. The good news is that God's forgiveness works much better than any eraser on the end of a pencil. When we come to Him, admitting our mistakes and asking for His help, He removes the sin "as far as the east is from the west"! If you tripped up today—in a big way or a small one—come to Him and ask for His help. Trust that God has forgiven you and choose to forgive your own mistakes as well.

Dear Lord,
it is so easy for me to make
mistakes, to do or say the wrong
thing, as I go about my day. I'm so
grateful for Your love and mercy
that brings me forgiveness and
removes my sin far away from me.
Help me to also forgive myself
and move on in Your grace.
Amen.

DISCUSSION PROMPT:

What do you need God to "erase" from your life today?

He's Always with You!

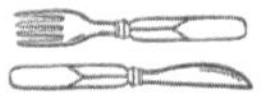

I can never escape from Your Spirit! I can never get away from Your presence! If I go up to heaven, You are there; if I go down to the grave, You are there. If I ride the wings of the morning, if I dwell by the farthest oceans, even there Your hand will guide me, and Your strength will support me.

PSALM 139:7–10 NLT

God has told us in His Word that He will never leave us! Isn't that amazing? No matter where we go, we will never be alone. Whenever we are afraid, He is right by our side. When we don't know what to do next, He is still with us, ready to guide us and make our way clear. When we are sad, He stands ready to comfort us. And in our happiest, most joyful moments, He is with us as well, sharing in the celebration.

There is no getting away from God—and why would you want to? He loves you so much—more than anyone else ever could. Delight in His nearness today and thank Him for always staying by your side. Ask Him for help whenever you need it and share your special moments with Him too. Share with Him whatever is on your heart today—He longs to hear from you!

Dear Lord,
no matter where I go, You are still with me. I am so grateful that no matter what I experience in my day, You have been with me—and You will be with me through all my tomorrows. Help me remember that I can always call on You whenever I need Your help.
Amen.

DISCUSSION PROMPT:

What happened in your day today that made you glad that God was with you?

He Knows What You Need

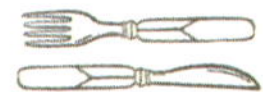

My God shall supply all your need according to His riches in glory by Christ Jesus.

PHILIPPIANS 4:19 NKJV

Do you ever worry about where you will live or where your next meal will come from? Most American families don't face these questions—although some do. What about other basic needs you have that go beyond your financial situation, things like our need for friendship, for purpose, for strength and good health? The Bible tells us that God will make sure we have everything we need, because we belong to Him through Christ Jesus. What a comfort that is to know!

God has blessed us with so much. And sometimes He even gives us things before we ask for them or before we even know we have a need. What do you need today? He stands ready to help. Even if all of your material and financial needs are met, He knows there are other things that are also necessary in life, and He has made provision for those too. Trust in Him—He won't let you down!

Dear Lord,
as a human being living on
this earth, I have so many needs.
Thank You for Your promise to
meet every need that I have—
sometimes even before I know the
need exists. You are a good God
who loves to care for His children,
and I'm so grateful for it.
Amen.

DISCUSSION PROMPT:

What needs do you have today that you are trusting the Lord to meet?

Peace and Quiet

I am leaving you with a gift—peace of mind and heart. And the peace I give is a gift the world cannot give. So don't be troubled or afraid.

JOHN 14:27 NLT

When was the last time you watched a baby sleeping? Or have you ever gone outside at night and realized that everything was quiet? When was the last time you just sat quietly in peace, with no sounds to bother you? These are moments of peace, and we all need them in our lives from time to time.

Most of us spend very little of our waking hours in silence. Too much noise is not good for our bodies or our stress levels. Spending two minutes in absolute silence is actually better for the brain than spending those two minutes listening to relaxing music. Sitting quietly in peace helps to lower our blood pressure and actually gives our brains a chance to restore themselves.

God loves peace! He loves it so much that it is one of the greatest gifts He offers to His children. Sometimes life is too busy or too noisy for us to calm down and tap into the peace that He gives. If that is the case, it's too busy and too noisy. In those times, ask God to bring His peace into your heart and thank Him for being the only Source of true peace.

Dear Lord,
life gets far too busy and
too noisy for me to rest in You
at times. I need Your peace every
day, all day long. As I seek to
follow You and Your will for my life,
help me to always rest in You and
Your peace when I need to.
Amen.

DISCUSSION PROMPT:

When was the last time you basked in the peace that Jesus offers? How can you rest in His peace today?

The Unchanging Rock

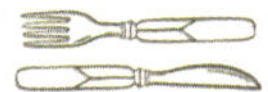

Trust in the LORD forever, for the LORD, the LORD himself, is the Rock eternal.

ISAIAH 26:4 NIV

What is the biggest object you have ever tried to move? Was it too heavy for you? What about the biggest rock you have ever seen? How heavy do you think it was? Rocks are known for being strong and secure, and the biggest ones are almost impossible to move.

When people talk about the person they trust the most, they will sometimes describe that person as "a rock" in their lives. One reason for this is that rocks don't move; they remain secure, in the same place, no matter what comes their way. In addition, rocks don't change. A rock that is put in a box and left there for many years will look exactly the same when the box is reopened.

The same is true for God. He does not change. He is immovable. No matter what we are going through, He will always stay the same: strong, steady, right beside us. He is always present, always caring, always delighted to spend time with us. He is bigger than any of our troubles or fears. We can count on Him to be faithful and good and trust Him to stay with us through every trouble and storm.

Dear Lord,
You are my rock. You are the unchanging and stable force in my life. I rely on You to stay with me, no matter what comes my way. I know You will always keep Your promises and You are always good. Thank You that I can cling to You even when things are changing around me.
Amen.

DISCUSSION PROMPT:

How does it make you feel to know that God will never change?

Succeeding in His Strength

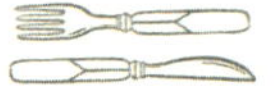

I can do all things through Christ,
because He gives me strength.

PHILIPPIANS 4:13 NCV

Before Abraham Lincoln ever became the sixteenth president of the United States, he faced many failures and challenges. He had lost eight elections, started two businesses that failed miserably, and had even experienced a nervous breakdown. And yet, he kept getting back up and moving forward in his life, eventually becoming one of the most important presidents in American history, leading the nation through the Civil War.

Whatever you have been through in your life—or even just in this day—you can have confidence that in everything God has called you to do, He will help you succeed. But this does not happen in your own strength—it happens as you learn to lean on Christ and on His strength working through you. When you really grasp that God's ways are perfect, that His plans for you are for your good, and that His promises are true, you will become bold and secure as you follow the path He has laid out for you.

Dear Lord,
I'm not always sure of where I'm going or what You are doing in my life. Help me to remember that everything You have called me to do, You will give me what I need to accomplish it. Thank You for being my strength this day and every day of my life.
Amen.

DISCUSSION PROMPT:

What do you need Christ's strength to accomplish today?

Running the Race

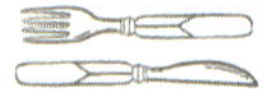

I have fought the good fight,
I have finished the race,
I have kept the faith.

II TIMOTHY 4:7 NCV

Have you ever run a marathon? What about a half marathon? For some of us, just jogging a mile or two around the neighborhood can feel like a really long race. When you have run a race of any real length, you usually get very tired. Some of us might even stop to walk in the middle for a bit when we feel like we just can't keep going.

Following God isn't always easy. In fact, He tells us that the road can be very difficult: "How narrow is the gate and difficult the road that leads to life, and few find it," Jesus said (Matthew 7:14 CSB). But living for Him is worth every last ounce of our energy. Maybe others have told you that it isn't worth it, but you know that it is. And Jesus encourages you to carry on. Be strong. Keep going. Don't give up! The race is still laid out in front of you, and the reward at the end is so worth it!

Dear Lord,

sometimes I grow weary in the race I am running for You. I know You want me to keep moving forward with everything I have to finish the race and win the prize. Help me to make it to the finish line with You. Amen.

DISCUSSION PROMPT:

In what area do you need determination today to keep going and not give up?

Mustard-Seed Faith

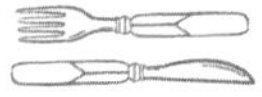

Then the disciples came to Jesus in private and asked, "Why couldn't we drive it out?" He replied, "Because you have so little faith. Truly I tell you, if you have faith as small as a mustard seed, you can say to this mountain, 'Move from here to there,' and it will move. Nothing will be impossible for you."

MATTHEW 17:19–21 NIV

Jesus tells us in the Bible that if we have faith the size of a mustard seed, we can do some pretty amazing things. Mustard seeds are incredibly small, measuring only one to two millimeters in diameter, which is about the size of the tip of a pencil. However, some mustard plants can grow up to nine feet tall. Mustard is the third most-used spice in the world after salt and pepper, and it has been around for a very long time. Some mustard seeds were found in a jar in China thought to be five thousand years old!

Sometimes life can be hard to understand, but our faith in God, Jesus says, doesn't have to be. It's simple. When we put faith in Him, He sees the goodness of Jesus in our lives instead of our sin, and He is able to forgive us. When troubles seem overwhelming and problems come at us from every direction, we can run straight to God. He has given us the gift of Jesus and faith the size of a mustard seed, and that is all we really need.

Dear Lord,
although my faith sometimes
seems small, I know it is enough
for You to use to move in my life.
I trust You to be with me always
and live through me each day.
Amen.

DISCUSSION PROMPT:

Do you have a lot of faith in Jesus or a little? How do you think your faith in Him could grow?

Always Faithful

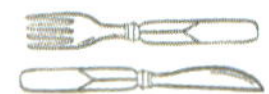

But the Lord is faithful, and he will strengthen you and protect you from the evil one.

II THESSALONIANS 3:3 NIV

Faithful friends are the best, aren't they? Their loyalty just can't be replaced. And what about a faithful pet, a dog that follows you through every room in the house just to be in your presence? Who doesn't love and appreciate that kind of loyalty?

Do you know who is even more faithful and loyal to you than your very best friend or your cherished pet? The Lord is. He will never leave you. Even if you feel as if you are in the middle of the most intense battle of your life, He will be right by your side, fighting with you. If people are saying unkind or untrue things about you, He will remind you of what He loves about you. If you feel as if nobody in the world cares about you, He will show you that He does. He will always help you find joy and peace in your life if you ask Him to do so. Delight in His nearness today and thank Him for staying close by your side. He loves to hear from you.

Dear Lord,
I am so thankful for Your faithfulness, Your willingness to stay by my side no matter what I face each day. Help me to rest in the knowledge that You are with me all the time.
Amen.

DISCUSSION PROMPT:

How do you feel knowing that God is always with you and never leaves your side?

Conversation Starters

What do you worry about the most?

What is the best name for a dog? For a cat? For an iguana?

What is the best thing and the worst thing about your position in the family birth order?

How are you generous?

If all of your wishes came true, what problems would it cause?

What's your favorite thing to do in the winter? In the summer?

Safe in His Care

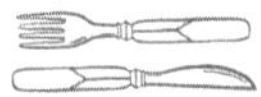

When I am afraid, I put my trust in you.
In God, whose word I praise, in God I trust;
I shall not be afraid. What can flesh do to me?

PSALM 56:3–4 ESV

Have you ever watched the old cartoons with a bird in a cage and a cat sitting just outside the cage watching the bird? Most of us have, and maybe some have even seen this take place in real life. If there was no cage, the bird would have every reason to be terrified, but because of the protective cage around it, the bird knows it is completely safe.

You, too, can feel as strong and as sure as that little bird inside of the cage because you have the best protection of all—your heavenly Father. There might be a cat just outside of the cage, waiting to pounce, but you can always trust that God is faithful, and He is taking good care of you. As a child of God, you can always count on Him to keep you safe. That doesn't mean there won't be times when you will be afraid or that you won't ever be hurt in life, but you can trust that God knows what is best for you and that He is watching out for you.

Dear Lord,
when the troubles of life come to my door and seem ready to pounce, I choose to trust in You. I never have to fear the evil things of this world. Thank You that You always watch out for me and keep me in Your constant, loving care.
Amen.

DISCUSSION PROMPT:

From what do you need protection today? How can God provide that protection for you?

Your Divine Purpose

And we know that God causes everything to work together for the good of those who love God and are called according to His purpose for them.

ROMANS 8:28 NLT

What are your hopes and dreams? What would be your ideal job? Maybe you have a list of exciting places you would like to visit, people you would like to meet, or a "bucket list" of fun activities you would like to do. All of these ideas are wonderful and good—God created this wonderful world, and He wants us to enjoy our time spent in it. But these questions don't answer the fundamental question that most of us ask ourselves sooner or later: *What is my purpose?*

Rest assured, God has a purpose for your life, a reason He created you just the way you are. And He wants you to do the things you love, but He wants you to do those things while you are loving Him and following Him and putting Him first in your life. You might not know yet what your specific purpose is, but as you follow Him, He will show you, especially as you continue to follow Him and choose to love Him with all your heart.

Dear Lord,
thank You that You have created me and placed me in this world filled with things I really enjoy. Help me to learn my true purpose in You, and to love You and serve You all of my days.
Amen.

DISCUSSION PROMPT:

What do you believe God wants you to do with your life? How are you fulfilling His purpose for you?

Secure Steps

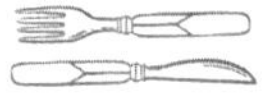

God arms me with strength, and He makes my way perfect. He makes me as surefooted as a deer, enabling me to stand on mountain heights.

PSALM 18:32–33 NLT

Have you ever watched a bighorn sheep climb along a rock face to reach a plant or blade of grass to eat? Without question, these sheep can nimbly climb, totally sure-footed, across nearly vertical surfaces that people wouldn't even think about traversing. They will calmly nibble their snack, then with agility and grace clamber back up the face of the rock without a second thought.

Just as bighorn sheep safely and nimbly navigate the faces of cliffs that we human beings would find treacherous, God will surely secure your footsteps throughout the most challenging parts of your life. He might not remove the danger; you might be walking across a precipice. But even when you think your way seems impossible, He is there to steady your footing and see you through. Ask Him today for a strong and sure foothold on whatever precipice you are climbing. He will secure your steps.

Dear Lord,
sometimes my way seems treacherous, and I feel like I could fall. Thank You for Your steady hand that helps me gain my footing again.
Amen.

DISCUSSION PROMPT:

Have you ever hit a rough patch and felt in danger of losing your footing? How did the Lord steady you in that moment?

Head for the Hills

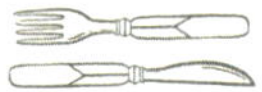

The LORD is my rock, my protection, my Savior.
My God is my rock. I can run to Him for safety.
He is my shield and my saving strength, my defender.

PSALM 18:2 NCV

When David was a young man, before he ever became the king of Israel, his father-in-law, King Saul, sought to kill him. The only place David could find safety was in the hills of Judea, outside of the cities, where he and his men took refuge in the cave of Adullam, which literally means "refuge" or "resting place." Here he could not only rest in physical safety, but he could also replenish himself spiritually as he turned to the Lord for help.

David's psalms are filled with references to God as a stronghold, a rock, a fortress, a refuge. He wrote many of these psalms when he was in danger or on the run. Where do you turn when you feel worried, stressed, or afraid? It is easy to take refuge in the things of this world—retail therapy, social media, binge-watching TV—but the best comfort is not found in any of those places. The greatest safety, comfort, and refuge is found in the Lord.

Dear Lord,
I come to You with so many concerns and problems that have crowded my day. Be my refuge as I lay my burdens at Your feet. Help me to trust in You.
Amen.

DISCUSSION PROMPT:

What does it mean to make God your stronghold? In what situation do you need to head for the hills and take shelter in Him?

Unshaken

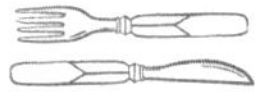

Since we are receiving a kingdom that cannot be shaken, let us be thankful. By it, we may serve God acceptably, with reverence and awe.

HEBREWS 12:28 CSB

Have you ever felt the tremors of an earthquake? It can be one of the most terrifying experiences a person can face, when the ground starts to violently shake and buildings collapse. Even living through an earthquake that causes only minimal damage can leave emotional scars of fear and terror that take many years to heal. Those feelings of fear and panic aren't always experienced by people in earthquakes; they can be triggered any time we feel the ground beneath our feet begin to shift metaphorically.

Maybe there are tremors happening in your life or your family today. Changes may be taking place in your finances, in your living situation, in a family member's health. Regardless of how bad the upheaval may become, you can keep your footing sure as you stay close to the Lord. You can stand firm even when all else shakes around you, because you are part of God's kingdom, which can never be shaken.

Dear Lord,
thank You for Your Word in Hebrews that reminds me that I am a part of Your kingdom, which will always stand firm. I draw strength and comfort from You, knowing that whatever happens in my life, You will always be by my side.
Amen.

DISCUSSION PROMPT:

When have you experienced a shaking in your life? How did the Lord see you through?

Under His Wings

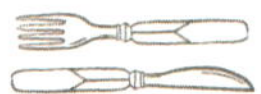

[God] watches over His nest like an eagle
and hovers over His young; He spreads His wings,
catches him, and carries him on His feathers.

DEUTERONOMY 32:11 CSB

There was once a barnyard cat that gave birth to six kittens, but unlike most mother cats, she didn't do much to care for them. She made sure they drank her milk a few times a day so they could survive, but that was about it. The kittens were lost and vulnerable—until the barnyard chicken took over. She cleaned the kittens and watched over them. They snuggled into her feathers just as they would have snuggled into their mother cat's fur. They didn't care that cats and chickens were usually natural enemies; they felt safe and secure when Mother Chicken stretched her wings of protection over them and kept them safe.

What a beautiful picture this is of what God does for us. Our loving heavenly Father longs to gather His children under His strong, incredible wings of protection. His love, grace, and mercy are stronger than any trouble or affliction that could come our way. And just like the barnyard kittens felt safe under the wings of Mother Chicken, we can also count on our Father to cover us with His wings of love and grace.

Dear Lord,
as I go about my day, it is easy
for me to forget that You are
always with me, ready to cover
me with Your grace and love.
As I face the pressures and demands
of this world, remind me always
to run to You. You will gather me
under Your wings of protection
and keep me safe from all harm.
I choose to rest in You.
Amen.

DISCUSSION PROMPT:

When have you felt the most "safe" and "protected" in your life? In what areas do you need to feel God's safety and protection today?

Losing Count

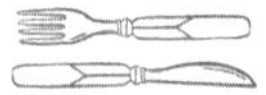

How precious are Your thoughts about me, O God. They cannot be numbered! I can't even count them; they outnumber the grains of sand! And when I wake up, You are still with me!

PSALM 139:17–18 NLT

The beach is one of God's most wonderful creations, wouldn't you agree? The sounds of waves crashing onto the shore, seagulls flying overhead, the smell of the salt water, the beauty of the seashells beneath your feet . . . And one of the best parts of all: squishing your toes down into the soft, cool grains of sand. The downside? All of those grains of sand can also get everywhere: in your swimsuit, between your toes, in your car, in your suitcase as you make your way back home.

No one has ever been able to count the grains of sand on even the smallest section of a beach. And the number of grains of sand in the entire world must be astronomical. Really, the number is so large it's uncountable. And the Bible says that's how many thoughts God has about you.

How overwhelming it is that the Creator of the entire universe—the One who made all of those grains of sand—is so in love with you, His beloved child, that He thinks of you that much! How could this knowledge change the way you live your life today?

Dear Lord,
I am entirely amazed to realize that Your thoughts toward me are truly infinite—utterly uncountable, like the grains of sand on the seashore. Thank You for loving me so tenaciously.
Amen.

DISCUSSION PROMPT:

How would a fresh understanding of God's passionate love for you change your circumstances today?

Thankful No Matter What

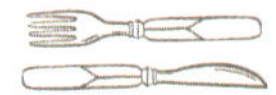

*Don't worry about anything; instead,
pray about everything. Tell God what you need,
and thank Him for all He has done.*

PHILIPPIANS 4:6 NLT

When Paul wrote the book of Philippians, do you know where he was writing from? Prison! He had been imprisoned, and his life was actually in danger because he refused to stop sharing the good news of Jesus. He wrote to his friends from his jail cell, sending them one of the most hopeful and joy-filled of all his letters. He told his friends in Philippi they shouldn't worry but instead pray—and more than that, they should be thankful to God for everything He had done for them, and for Paul.

As people living on a fallen earth, we go through many different situations that cause worry and fear: challenges at work or in school, sickness, relationship troubles or divorce, financial difficulties; even moving to a new house or starting a new job can cause anxiety. When we come to God and lay our burdens at His feet, we can rest assured that He is taking care of us. Tell Him what you need today, be thankful for what He has given—no matter what you are facing—and watch Him take care of the rest.

Dear Lord,
it's easy to get worried and upset when I look at the world around me. Some days problems seem to multiply faster than I can solve them. And yet, I am so thankful for the ways I can see You working in my life. Help me to always trust in You, that You know what You are doing and You have great plans for my life.
Amen.

DISCUSSION PROMPT:

What are the greatest worries on your mind? What can you be thankful for in the midst of these concerns?

Happily Ever After

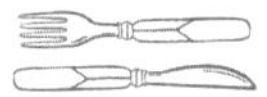

God will bless you hungry people.
You will have plenty to eat!
God will bless you people
who are now crying. You will laugh!

LUKE 6:21 CEV

We all love a happy ending, don't we? When the prince sweeps the girl off her feet and then takes her off to live in the castle . . . When the underdog baseball team wins the championship . . . When the hero rides off into the sunset . . . Everything turns out wonderful in the end—in the movies. In real life? Not so much.

The reason most of us hope for movies to have happily-ever-after endings is because we long for that same type of ending in our own real-life stories. Unfortunately, in this world without God's grace and intervention, that is not guaranteed. One of God's most precious promises is that we can trust Him to write a happy ending to our story. Regardless of how painful or difficult life gets, we know that for those who love Him, one day everything will turn out all right. He will wipe every tear from our eyes, and pain will no longer exist (Revelation 21:4). That's the real happily-ever-after we long for—and you have God's promise that you will gain it in the end.

Dear Lord,
sometimes things just don't work out the way I want them to. Help me to remember always that You have a plan, and You are working it out for my ultimate good. And I look forward to the best happily-ever-after in heaven, where I will see You face-to-face.
Amen.

DISCUSSION PROMPT:

What is your favorite happily-ever-after moment in a movie or book? How does it remind you of your heavenly future, where the best happily-ever-after will ultimately take place?

Group Activity

I'M SO THANKFUL!

Make a list of the things each member of the family is most thankful for. If you'd like, add drawings, photographs, or pictures from magazines or advertisements to create a "Grateful Collage." Hang the list or collage somewhere in your home where everyone can see it and remember to thank God for all His many blessings.

Turning Sad into Glad

You have turned for me my mourning into dancing; you have loosed my sackcloth and clothed me with gladness, that my glory may sing your praise and not be silent. O LORD my God, I will give thanks to you forever!

PSALM 30:11–12 ESV

In the Old Testament, people wore black garments when they wanted to publicly express their grief over a lost loved one or their extreme distress over a tragedy that had befallen them. These garments were made of sackcloth, a coarse, inexpensive material made from the hair of black goats. Someone who was in this period of mourning would refrain from attending any festivities, instead publicly weeping and wearing only the black sackcloth garments. When the time of mourning was over, however, they would set aside those mourning clothes, dress themselves in their usual outfits again, and reengage with society.

In Psalm 30, David used this practice as an analogy to show the difference that God had made in his heart. His deepest grief, his greatest lament, had been turned into a time of dancing and joy. If you are facing a disappointment, aggravation, calamity, or

even deep sadness or discouragement, God can help you with those feelings. He can change your sad into glad, your black clothes of sackcloth into beautiful garments of colorful joy.

Dear Lord,
whatever sadness or distress
I am feeling today, I give to You.
Turn my lament into dancing, my
sad into glad, as I trust You to work
out Your purpose in my life.
Amen.

DISCUSSION PROMPT:

What sad situation in your life needs to be turned to glad? How can you focus on God's goodness in the midst of the situation today?

God Is for You!

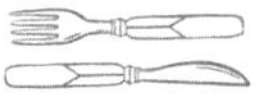

Having chosen them, He called them to come to Him. And having called them, He gave them right standing with Himself. And having given them right standing, He gave them His glory. What shall we say about such wonderful things as these? If God is for us, who can ever be against us?

ROMANS 8:30–31 NLT

For years, William Wilberforce pushed the British Parliament to abolish slavery. Discouraged, he was about to give up, when his elderly friend John Wesley heard of it and from his deathbed asked for a pen and sheet of paper to write to Wilberforce:

"Unless God has raised you up for this very thing, you will be worn out by the opposition of men and devils. But if God be for you, who can be against you? Are all of them stronger than God? Oh be not weary of well-doing! Go on, in the name of God and in the power of his might, till even American slavery shall vanish away before it."

Wesley died six days after writing those words, but Wilberforce fought forty-five more years until, three days before his own death in 1833, slavery was abolished in Great Britain.

What has God raised you up to do? If He is for you, there is no one and nothing that can stand against you. Set aside any discouragement and keep moving forward. He is with you!

Dear Lord,
it is always good to be
reminded to keep moving
forward in the things You have
called me to do. Help me not to
get discouraged or lose my focus on
the purposes You have for my life.
Amen.

DISCUSSION PROMPT:

What is God calling you to do today?
How will you need His help
to follow through?

The Master Potter

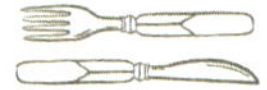

But now, O Lord, You are our Father;
we are the clay, and You our potter;
and all we are the work of Your hand.

ISAIAH 64:8 NKJV

Have you ever tried to create something out of clay on a potter's wheel? It isn't easy. In the hands of an amateur, even the best-intentioned one, the "works of art" often turn out crude and lopsided. It takes real skill to craft something out of humble clay, something that is useful or beautiful, something worthy of being saved, kept, even treasured.

The Bible depicts God as the Master Potter. He has lovingly formed you in His hands just as a potter shapes the clay on his wheel. Psalm 139 says that it is He who has created your inward parts, He who knit you together in your mother's womb. Unlike mere humans, whose mistakes are many, God doesn't make mistakes with the clay on His wheel. You have been remarkably and wonderfully created by His hands, and He longs to continue His hands-on work in your life.

Dear Lord,
You are my Creator, the One who knit me together in my mother's womb, the One who knows me inside and out. I invite Your continuing work in my life and my heart. Be as hands-on as You would like to be in everything that concerns me.
Amen.

DISCUSSION PROMPT:

Do you agree that you have been wonderfully made? How does God's ongoing and intentional molding of your life make you feel?

Tethered to the Lord

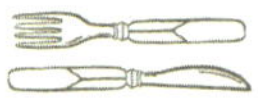

But now, O Jacob, listen to the Lord who created you. O Israel, the one who formed you says, "Do not be afraid, for I have ransomed you. I have called you by name; you are Mine. When you go through deep waters, I will be with you. When you go through rivers of difficulty, you will not drown. When you walk through the fire of oppression, you will not be burned up; the flames will not consume you."

ISAIAH 43:1–2 NLT

In July 2018, twelve young boys and their coach set out after soccer practice to spend some time exploring the caves of Tham Luang, Thailand. But while they were deep underground, a heavy rain blew in, trapping them and instigating a massive, eighteen-day search-and-rescue operation whose drama played out on televisions worldwide. Ultimately, in order to be rescued, each boy was tethered to a diver, who shared oxygen with him and dragged him along through the cold, murky water. All each boy had to do in order to be rescued was to lie still and completely trust the diver to deliver him safely to the other side.

God is a lot like that diver. He will stay tethered to you as He guides you through the difficult terrain and challenges of life. You don't need to be afraid. Just as the divers shared their lifegiving oxygen with the boys, God Himself will provide everything you need to make it through, and He will guide you safely to the other side.

Dear Lord.
I am so thankful for Your
guidance and care in the difficult
and challenging passages of my life.
Keep leading me and guiding me.
I will walk by Your side until I am
safely on the other side.
Amen.

DISCUSSION PROMPT:

How can you tether yourself securely to God today?

The God of All Comfort

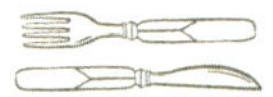

[God] comforts us every time we have trouble, so when others have trouble, we can comfort them with the same comfort God gives us. We share in the many sufferings of Christ. In the same way, much comfort comes to us through Christ.

II CORINTHIANS 1:4–5 NCV

The apostle Paul had to deal with far more trouble than most of us could imagine. He was imprisoned, beaten, stoned, and shipwrecked. His enemies literally wanted to kill him. He faced danger everywhere he went as he worked to spread the gospel, and he experienced significant hardships without adequate food, money, or clothing much of the time.

Still, whenever Paul's troubles began to get him down and discouragement threatened to creep in, God was his comfort. The words Paul wrote in II Corinthians 1, he wrote from experience. But the comfort he received didn't equate to a soft bed with a comfy pillow to sleep on at night. The Greek word he used for "comfort" is more closely associated with our English word *courage*. Paul received the courage he needed from the Lord to keep on keeping on.

Your life is no doubt much different from Paul's experiences, but you likely face difficulties from time to time. Isn't it good to know that whenever you feel the weight and the burden of your problems, you can find comfort in God? He cares about everything you are going through, and His comfort will strengthen you and give you courage to see it through.

Dear Lord,
I need Your comfort—Your courage—to fill me today as I face the challenges that life has brought my way. I'm so grateful for the way You comfort Your children, even in the midst of difficulty.
Amen.

DISCUSSION PROMPT:

Why is God's comfort so important during times of struggle? In what situation do you most need God's courage and comfort today?

Our Compassionate God

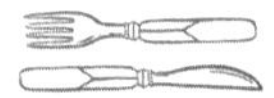

Praise be to the God and Father of our Lord Jesus Christ, the Father of compassion and the God of all comfort.

II CORINTHIANS 1:3 NIV

The Bible tells us that, unlike the capricious ancient gods worshiped by pagan nations, the God we worship is filled with compassion. Not only that, He is the "Father of compassion." Compassion is a feeling of deep sympathy and sorrow for someone who has been stricken by misfortune, along with a powerful desire to alleviate that suffering. God not only sees the plight of human beings, but He is also moved to intervene. That is why He sent His Son, Jesus, to the earth—to save us and restore us to Himself.

Compassion is what moved Jesus to heal diseases and infirmities, cast out demons, raise the dead, forgive sins, and make broken people whole again. Matthew 9:36 tells us, "When he saw the crowds, he felt compassion for them" (NIV).

Don't think for a second that God is indifferent or unconcerned about what you are going through. He sees your hurts and your struggles. His heart is filled with empathy and compassion for you, and He longs to help. Because of His great compassion, you can count on Him to intervene when you come to Him in your time of need.

Dear Lord,
Your compassion overwhelms me when I consider who I am and who You are. I'm so grateful that You care about every detail of my life and that I can come to You in my time of need. Help me always remember to seek You first.
Amen.

DISCUSSION PROMPT:

Have you ever wondered whether God was indifferent toward the difficulties and challenges in your life? How does it make you feel to know how much He cares and is moved with compassion for you?

He Hears You

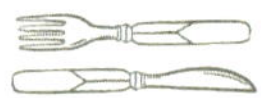

Because He bends down to listen,
I will pray as long as I have breath!

PSALM 116:2 NLT

Have you ever felt as though the prayers you pray hit the ceiling and bounce right back down to the floor? When you have prayed and shared your heartfelt needs with the Lord, are there times when you feel as if you are met with . . . only . . . silence? How can you know that God hears you when you call out to Him—*really* hears you? The answer lies in His Word.

There are those times when God moves mightily in your life, answering prayers in unexpected ways you never dreamed were possible, but when *this* prayer you are praying isn't one of *those* times, be encouraged: He does hear you. He has turned His ear to you. He loves you and He is there. Even when He seems to be silent, He is often working behind the scenes to make a way for you where there seems to be no way. Consider how many of God's people cried out to Him in Scripture: Moses, who longed to free God's people from slavery; David, while being chased by his enemies and hiding in caves; Hannah, who desperately wanted a child. All of them went through a period of silence, of

waiting, before God's promises were fulfilled in their lives.

God hears you. He knows what your family needs, and He is listening, waiting to provide, waiting to respond in love and in grace.

Dear Lord,
it's so reassuring to be reminded
of the promises in Your Word that
You will always hear me when I call
out to You. Hear me today. I trust
that You are working everything out
in my life for Your good purpose.
Amen.

DISCUSSION PROMPT:

What prayer are you waiting for God to answer in your life? How easy—or difficult—has it been to wait for His response?

What's New with You?

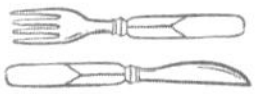

Now we look inside, and what we see is that anyone united with the Messiah gets a fresh start, is created new. The old life is gone; a new life emerges!

II CORINTHIANS 5:17 THE MESSAGE

Have you ever tried to break a bad habit? Maybe you wanted to lose weight, eat better, exercise more, stop texting while driving . . . The list of things you want to change about yourself could go on and on. And we all know how difficult it can be to make those new habits last any longer than a few weeks.

The good news is that the greatest change of all happened when we accepted Jesus as our Savior and made Him the Lord of our lives. He loves us just the way we are—but He has also given us His Spirit to work inside of our hearts to make us more and more like Himself. As believers in Him, we are new creations, and we can be set free from old patterns and the failures of the past. Living each day in the Holy Spirit's strength enables us to move forward in life, walking each day with Him as He helps us embrace the "new." Allow Him to move in your heart today and do a new thing in your life!

Dear Lord,
I am excited to see what new thing You want to do within me. Help me to stay open to the leading of Your Spirit this day and every day.
Amen.

DISCUSSION PROMPT:

How has God done a new thing in your life in the past? What is He doing today?

A Safe Space

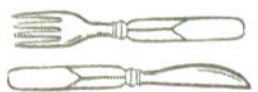

The name of the LORD is a fortified tower; the righteous run to it and are safe.

PROVERBS 18:10 NIV

These days there is a lot of talk about finding a "safe space"—a place where people can go to feel safe, obviously, but also to be heard, understood, and unconditionally loved by the people who are there. When the home is a "safe space," everyone is free to be themselves, to express their needs and hopes and dreams without judgment, and to love one another and be loved in return. In this world filled with imperfect people, we don't provide each other with a completely safe space all the time, but a family that seeks to maintain a safe space for all its members is a family that is growing in love and grace.

The safest space we could ever find is revealed in the words of Proverbs 18:10. Wherever we seek safety—whether it be physical or emotional or spiritual—it is God's presence with us in that place that truly provides the strength and protection that we need. Even if your earthly "safe spaces" fail you now and again, God's presence never will. He is always ready to listen, and He understands what is in your heart. Let Him be your safest space today.

Dear Lord,
thank You for Your presence
that is always with me. In a world
filled with imperfect people,
You are the safest place to be.
Amen.

DISCUSSION PROMPT:

In what space do you feel the safest? Maybe it's your bedroom, your car, at church, or with a friend. How does God meet you in that place?

Conversation Starters

What is one thing you would like to know about the future?

What do you admire the most about your parents?

What do you ride first at an amusement park?

If you could have any view from your window, what would it be?

What are your best qualities?

What's the story behind your name?

Even Better Than Flowers!

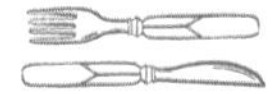

The grass withers, the flower fades,
but the word of our God will stand forever.

ISAIAH 40:8 ESV

What parent or grandparent hasn't received a hand-picked bouquet of flowers from their son or daughter or grandchild, who didn't treasure it as the most beautiful flower arrangement in the world? Picked with loving care by chubby hands and presented with an "I love you, Mommy," even if they are made up of weeds or grass, these bouquets are cherished and held dear for as long as they last—because of the love of the one who gave them.

The Bible tells us that God's love is like that, too, and even though the flowers and other treasures we receive in this world don't last, His Word—His timeless love letter to us—will endure forever. Even as we face uncertainty, difficulties, and problems, we are reminded of His unchanging love and character that is revealed in Scripture. It will never wilt, fade, or crumble, and as we put our trust in the promises it reveals, He proves His love and grace to us over and over again.

Dear Lord,
I'm so grateful for Your Word,
Your living love letter to me.
In it, You show me who You are
and how much You care for me.
Thank You that it never changes
and will endure forever.
Amen.

DISCUSSION PROMPT:

What is your favorite promise from God's Word? What makes it your favorite?

Come On In!

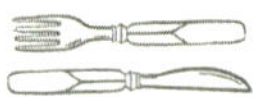

Let us come boldly to the throne of our gracious God. There we will receive His mercy, and we will find grace to help us when we need it most.

HEBREWS 4:16 NLT

A man and his wife were sound asleep in their bed when suddenly the door to their room opened and a young fellow crept inside. He had walked around the bed to the man's side before the woman was startled awake.

If this trespasser had been a stranger to the couple, this would have been a felony—criminal breaking and entering. If he had been a friend of the couple's, just walking into their bedroom in the middle of the night would have been downright rude. But the intruder was the couple's four-year-old son, who crawled into the bed and declared, "I want to sleep in the middle." The father and mother gladly opened their arms, touched by the need for their child to be comforted by their presence.

Just as a child is welcome in his parents' presence, we are welcome in the presence of our heavenly Father. Hebrews 4:16 tells us we can approach God's throne of grace "with confidence." We can come to Him with the secure knowledge that He cares for us, He delights in spending time with us, He wants to meet our needs (see I Peter 5:7). Don't be afraid to approach Him with anything on your mind. Instead, come to Him with the boldness of a child who knows he is completely loved and entirely wanted by his Father.

Dear Lord,
sometimes, like a child who needs his parents in the middle of the night, I need to come to You, just to be loved and cared for and reassured that everything will be all right. Thank You for always welcoming me with open arms. Amen.

DISCUSSION PROMPT:

How confident are you when you approach your heavenly Father? How would a fresh understanding of His love for you affect how you pray?

Family Recipes

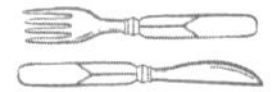

Remember the days of old; consider the generations long past. Ask your father and he will tell you, your elders, and they will explain to you.

DEUTERONOMY 32:7 NIV

Does your family have a secret recipe—maybe a special way your great-grandmother cooked a dish that has now been passed down through the generations? For some families, it's a certain way the dressing is fixed with the turkey at Thanksgiving, or it could be the baked beans or Jell-O fruit salad brought each year to the family picnic. Maybe it's a special dessert only prepared during the holidays.

Whatever it is, it's so important to have those family recipes written down so they aren't forgotten or lost for future generations. Even more important, though, is passing down the legacy of faith that we have received from the Lord. God intends that we share His mighty acts with the generations that follow us—both the stories of His works found in Scripture and the stories of what He has done personally in our own lives. Just as Moses instructed the people to pass on the legacy of God's miraculous deeds, from the elders to the children and young men and women, we also must share the stories of our own salvation and the ways the Lord has helped us to face challenges and difficulties in His strength. The psalmist wrote: "Even when I am old and gray, do not forsake me, my God, till I declare your power to the next generation, your mighty acts to all who are to come" (Psalm 71:18 NIV). When this happens, we pass the faith along—an even greater legacy than Grandma's recipe for pumpkin pie!

Dear Lord,
You have done amazing deeds—
both for Your people in the Bible
and in my own life. Help me to
live in such a way that I will pass
the legacy of faith on to my own
children and generations to come.
Amen.

DISCUSSION PROMPT:

Does your family have a secret recipe? What about a spiritual legacy? How could you begin today to create a legacy of faith within your family?

Being Cheerful

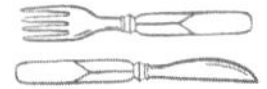

This is the day the Lord has made;
we will rejoice and be glad in it.

PSALM 118:24 NKJV

The story of Pollyanna told the adventures of an optimistic young girl who always made the choice to be cheerful no matter what bad things happened around her. Today we might call someone a "Pollyanna" if they are overly lighthearted in the midst of challenges and problems—but when we think about it, isn't that a better way to approach life? In almost every situation, we have the choice to look at the downside or the upside of whatever we face. Of course, it is good to be realistic and face the problems that need to be faced, but when suffering comes our way, God is pleased when we find ways to be thankful anyway (see I Thessalonians 5:16–18). Even if the only thing we can be thankful for is that He is with us—that is enough!

When you trust in God's goodness, you will find gladness. No matter what you are going through today, look for the good in the situation. Draw near to the Father and ask Him to give you a cheerful heart.

Dear Lord,
it is good to be cheerful and find the good in whatever situation I face. In those times when it's hard to be optimistic, help me to see the circumstances through Your eyes and trust in You to make all things right.
Amen.

DISCUSSION PROMPT:

Are you a cheerless or an optimistic person? How does your attitude affect the way you view the problems you face in life?

A Work in Progress

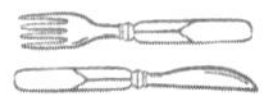

I have done my best in the race,
I have run the full distance,
and I have kept the faith.

II TIMOTHY 4:7 GNT

Have you ever heard the phrase, "It's the journey that counts, not the destination"? Sometimes the process of getting somewhere or achieving something is as important and transformational as the final result. And God is all about the process of transformation in our lives.

Let's face it. None of us is perfect, and we won't be until we get to heaven. But as we humbly come before the Lord, He will continue to transform our hearts to be more and more like His—hearts of love and compassion and grace, both toward others and toward ourselves. When the circumstances of life bring stressors or adjustments we need to make, He will help us make those changes through His Spirit that lives within us. And as we do so, we will come to more truly love one another. Sure, heaven will be wonderful someday, when we will all live in perfect love and harmony, but don't forget that the journey to get there counts too. And He will be with us every step of the way.

Dear Lord,
I can't wait to get to heaven someday to be with You and live in perfect peace and love forever. Until that day comes, though, I want to live my life here on earth honoring You and the transformation You are bringing about in my heart. Thank You for the work You are doing in my life. Amen.

DISCUSSION PROMPT:

What was the last road trip that you took? How did the "journey" compare to the "destination"? How is God transforming you through your journey through this life to prepare you for your ultimate destination in heaven?

The Best Inheritance

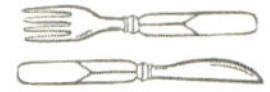

I remember your genuine faith,
for you share the faith that first filled
your grandmother Lois and your mother, Eunice.
And I know that same faith continues strong in you.

II TIMOTHY 1:5 NLT

Even though Grandma and Grandpa Jones didn't have much money, they always made the holidays special for their grandchildren. There was always lots of good food, games, laughter, and love—and they always made sure their family knew the real reason for the season wasn't presents or what could be found in their stockings: The reason for the celebration was because of Jesus and what He had done for them. Grandma and Grandpa Jones might not have given the most expensive gifts, and they might not have left a large inheritance behind when they passed away, but they left a rich spiritual inheritance for the ones they loved the most.

The Bible tells us about Timothy's grandma, Lois, and his mother, Eunice, who shared their genuine faith and relationship with the Lord with Timothy. Their influence on his life prepared him for the life and ministry that God later had for him.

Preparing this spiritual inheritance for the ones God places in our care is possible when we live in close communion with Him and when we actively share His work in our lives with those we love. How are you demonstrating your faith and love for God to your loved ones today? What kind of lasting legacy will you leave?

Dear Lord,
I'm grateful for the spiritual inheritance I have been given through You. Help me to pass the legacy of faith on to those whom You have placed in my care. Guide us and teach us all as we strive to live for You.
Amen.

DISCUSSION PROMPT:

Have you ever received an inheritance? What did it consist of? What can you do to pass on a spiritual inheritance to those you love?

A New Name

[Jesus said,] "I tell you that you are Peter, and on this rock I will build my church, and the gates of Hades will not overcome it."

MATTHEW 16:18 NIV

We know Peter to be one of Jesus' closest followers, but he wasn't always that way—in fact, he wasn't always named Peter. Before he met Jesus, his name was Simon, and he was a fisherman known for his brash speech and impulsive behavior. After meeting Jesus, the Lord gave Simon a new name—and it wasn't chosen randomly. Jesus named this follower of His Cephas—"Peter" in our English language—which means "the rock." Eventually Peter lived up to this new name by becoming one of Jesus' most enthusiastic, wholehearted followers, but throughout his time with Jesus, he had a lot to learn. He disagreed with Jesus (Matthew 16:22–23), cut a man's ear off with a sword (John 18:10–11), and even denied knowing Jesus after the Lord's arrest (John 18:15–27). But later in the book of Acts, after the Spirit came to live in Peter's heart and worked to transform him, he became the rock of the early church, spreading the gospel and writing letters read by believers around the world even today.

Just as He did with Peter, Jesus has given each of His followers a new name and identity. By believing in Him, we become a Christian (see Acts 11:26), which means "Christ-one." And as we follow Him, we become more and more like Him as His Spirit works in our hearts.

Dear Lord,
I'm so grateful You have called me to follow You and given me a new name and a new identity. Help me to always live up to it as I allow Your Holy Spirit to work in my heart and my life.
Amen.

DISCUSSION PROMPT:

If you could change your name today, would you? If so, what would you change it to and why?

You Are So Worth It!

God paid a great price for you.

I CORINTHIANS 6:20 CEV

Little children don't always understand the price of the toys, clothes, and other items their parents purchase for them. Have you ever bought a new flashy toy for a baby, only when they opened the gift, they were more interested in playing with the bow or the wrapping paper? If you buy a toddler a pair of expensive boots, they may be excited about wearing them for a day but the next day put their old, ragtag tennis shoes back on before going out to play. It's enough to make a parent sigh and say, "I sure wish kids knew what things cost!"

Now it's obvious a child can't appreciate all the things a parent does for him and the sacrifices his family makes to give him nice things, and that's the way it's supposed to be. A loving parent enjoys providing for their children, but when the child grows up, he learns to value what he was given and be thankful for it.

God loves to lavish His children with wonderful gifts, as well. James 1:17 tell us: "Every good and perfect gift is from above, coming down from the Father of the heavenly lights" (NIV). But

the greatest gift He could ever give was the gift of His own dear Son, Jesus—and what a price He paid. The cost of our salvation was the highest price ever paid: "the precious blood of Christ, a lamb without blemish or defect" (I Peter 1:19 NIV). When Jesus gave His life in our place, He did so willingly, because God deemed each one of us *worth it.* Now that you know the cost of your life in Him, will you thank Him for it?

Dear heavenly Father,
I am so thankful and blessed to be Your child. Words cannot express how much I love You and how grateful I am for the gift of Your Son. Help me to live a life worthy of His sacrifice for me.
Amen.

DISCUSSION PROMPT:

What is the most expensive gift you have ever received? What about the most meaningful gift? How would a greater appreciation of what Jesus did for you change the way you live your life?

Passing Through the Waters

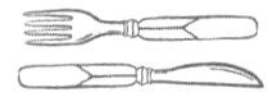

When you pass through the waters, I will be with you; and through the rivers, they shall not overwhelm you.

ISAIAH 43:2 ESV

Have you ever taken a child through an automatic car wash for the first time? No matter how much you try to prepare them for the experience, it can be quite frightening! As you check that the windows are up (and double-check!) and ease the car toward the wash, the automated tracks pull the car forward, closer and closer to the cave-like cocoon of darkness ahead. Soap is quietly sprayed all around, but when the thunderous rush of water and brushes attack the car from all directions? That's when the terror usually hits, and your toddler wants out of the vehicle—NOW!

It's usually better to wait a few years past toddlerhood to put your child through such an experience! By the time they are in elementary school, many kids beg to go through the exciting experience of the automatic car wash. Thankfully, at the end of every chaotic pummeling of soap, water, and giant brushes, the plumes of water cease and your car is propelled back out into the sunshine of the outside world, shiny and clean.

When the stormy, pummeling circumstances of life try to overwhelm us and things feel out of control, we can sometimes feel like that toddler in the car wash, screaming, "I want out NOW!" If we wait patiently, though, and realize that our loving Parent is still with us, still in the driver's seat, we know we will pass through the waters and into the sunshine at the other side, a shiny and clean example of His protection and grace.

Dear Lord,
sometimes I feel like I am in the middle of a car wash that is out of my control. The chaos and turmoil can be scary. Help me to look for You in these times and remember that with You, I have nothing to fear, that You will bring me safely through to the other side.
Amen.

DISCUSSION PROMPT:

What "car wash experience" have you endured in your life? How did God show His faithfulness to you in that experience?

Group Activity

JIGSAW PUZZLE

Have a family puzzle night. (Or, if your family doesn't like jigsaws, have a LEGO night.) Look at how all the pieces fit together to make a beautiful masterpiece when it is finished. Each piece is different, but each piece is important to the final product—just like each of us is unique and important in God's family.

The Little Things

Every good action and every perfect gift is from God. These good gifts come down from the Creator of the sun, moon, and stars, who does not change like their shifting shadows.

JAMES 1:17 NCV

Sarah had been homebound for several months due to some medical issues, and she was missing the fellowship of her church family. One day her adult son stopped by to see her, and he shared with her that she could access her church's worship services on her computer. When he showed her how to join the live broadcast the next Sunday, Sarah was overjoyed. In the midst of her illness, she was so thankful for the blessing of joining with her church family in worshiping God.

Sarah had a thankful heart. Despite the limitations of her current situation, she was thankful for even the little blessings that God brought into her life. In Psalm 116:3, the psalmist shared his situation—likely an illness of some sort: "The cords of death entangled me" (NIV). But he still had a thankful heart and blessed the Lord for being gracious and showing him compassion when he was "brought low" (verses 5–6 NIV).

It can be difficult to find ways to be grateful when we are facing sickness or other troubles. But if we can look up past the challenges, we will see the Giver of all good gifts is ready to bless us—in large ways and in small. And we will learn to give Him thanks—even in the little things.

Dear Lord,
You are always helping me, blessing me, giving me wonderful gifts. Help me to pay attention to the many ways You pour Your grace and kindness into my life. I'm so thankful!
Amen.

DISCUSSION PROMPT:

Name a little thing for which you can thank God today.

Face-to-Face Friendship with God

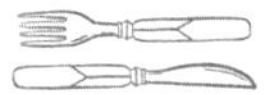

The Lord would speak to Moses face to face, just like a friend.

EXODUS 33:11 CEV

With all the electronic devices, smartphones, iPads, and laptops, the world is more connected than it has ever been—but more and more, we seem to have lost the face-to-face contact we used to have. During the Covid-19 pandemic, Zoom meetings took the place of in-person classrooms or conference tables, and weddings, birthday parties, even funerals were postponed or downsized to have the fewest number of people in attendance.

Let's "face" it (pun intended). Nothing can take the place of family and friends getting together in person, sharing with each other face-to-face. Did you know that God feels the same? He used to walk with Adam and Eve in the garden before sin came into the world, and He spoke with His servant Moses face-to-face, "as one speaks to a friend." God so longed for a relationship with His children that He sent Jesus to make it possible for us to return to His presence, and today, just as Jesus offered His disciples a close, intimate, face-to-face relationship, we also can have that close, amazing friendship with God. Maybe it's time for a get-together with Him!

Dear Lord,
it's mind-blowing to know that You, the Creator of the entire universe, so wanted to be friends with me that You sent Jesus to earth to make our relationship possible. Help me never to take my friendship with You for granted, but to cherish it and share it with others.
Amen.

DISCUSSION PROMPT:

When you hear the word friend, what comes to mind? Maybe someone who knows all your secrets? Maybe someone who enjoys your company, and whose company you enjoy? What does it mean to you to view God as your friend, someone who wants to spend time with you face-to-face?

The Easy Yoke

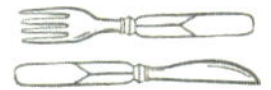

[Jesus said], "Take My yoke upon you. Let Me teach you, because I am humble and gentle at heart, and you will find rest for your souls."

MATTHEW 11:29 NLT

A Sunday school teacher once read Matthew 11:29 to a class of young children, and then asked the question: "Jesus told us that His yoke is easy. Does anyone here know what a 'yoke' is?" One of the boys in the class raised his hand and confidently stated, "A yoke is a piece of wood they put around the necks of animals so they can help each other out."

The teacher nodded and then asked, "What is the yoke that Jesus puts on us?" One of the quieter girls in the class raised her hand and then said, "It is when God puts His own arm around us."

When Jesus came, He offered an "easy" yoke to bear—compared to the rules and regulations of the religious leaders of that time. They had put "heavy burdens" on the people that were virtually impossible to keep (Matthew 23:4). Jesus offers us a better way. In our efforts to please God, He is there to help. He comes beside us, puts His arm around us, and makes it possible to live a life that is pleasing to God. And when we mess up, He has made the way possible for forgiveness and grace. Do you need Jesus' yoke instead of the burdens you carry? He is ready to put His arm around you today.

Dear Lord,
sometimes I work so hard in my own efforts to please You and do everything I should. But You remind me that You don't want me to carry a heavy burden on my own. Thank You for putting Your arm around me and seeing me through.
Amen.

DISCUSSION PROMPT:

What other "yokes" have you carried recently? How do they compare with the yoke Jesus provides?

Beautiful Images

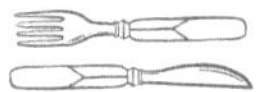

All of us are looking with unveiled faces at the glory of the Lord as if we were looking in a mirror. We are being transformed into that same image from one degree of glory to the next degree of glory. This comes from the Lord, who is the Spirit.

II CORINTHIANS 3:18 CEB

It can be so fun to look through old family photo albums, can't it? As you peer at old black-and-white images, you look to find a part of yourself in the photos of your great-grandparents, or kids might try to match their physical characteristics to those in pictures of their mom or dad at the same age. What really stands out are the more unusual traits: the big ears, the crooked teeth, even a cowlick or unruly curls on the head of a past relative.

In addition to the physical genetic traits we've received from our family, we also learn character traits from them. Honesty, patience, generosity—these things can be taught to even the youngest members of the family, just as the negative traits can be picked up, such as short-temperedness, selfishness, or greed. People will try all kinds of ways to change the physical traits they don't like about themselves—wearing makeup, enduring braces on their teeth—but transforming our character into the image of Jesus is far more valuable. Isn't it wonderful that the Holy Spirit is constantly working in our lives to make us more like Him?

Dear Lord,
when I look in the mirror, I see things I like and don't like about my appearance. Even more important than what I look like physically, though, is what You see when You look at my heart. Keep working in my life to make me more like You.
Amen.

DISCUSSION PROMPT:

What physical traits run in your family? What about character traits? How is your family growing together to be more like Jesus?

Everlasting Love

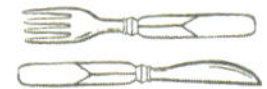

How precious is Your unfailing love, O God!
All humanity finds shelter in the shadow of Your wings.

PSALM 36:7 NLT

I'm done!" Jacob cried as he slammed the door. He'd had it with his friend Mark, who had hurt his feelings—again. The friendship just wasn't worth it anymore, and Jacob decided it was over.

That's how many human relationships work—when we reach the limits of our goodwill or patience in putting up with another person's rudeness or bad behavior, we cut them off and our love reaches its end. Human beings are sinful and frequently unfaithful, and although we may try to love other people perfectly, we often fail at the task.

Not so for God! The Bible tells us that God's love has no limits. That means no matter what we could ever do, He won't—He can't—stop loving us! Paul wrote these words to describe this ideal love, God's love: "Love never gives up, never loses faith, is always hopeful, and endures through ever circumstance" (I Corinthians 13:7 NLT). God's love is a love we can count on. Even when tough times come and we think He has somehow failed us, He hasn't. As God's children, we can be sure that no matter what happens to us, God is constantly loving us in it and through it, and He will love us on the other side of it as well. His love will never fail.

Dear Lord,
Your love is amazing,
everlasting, and life-changing.
Even when other people fail me
or disappoint me, I'm so grateful
I can always count on You!
Amen.

DISCUSSION PROMPT:

Have you ever wanted to stop loving another person? What happened? How is God's love different from your own in that situation?

I'm Stuffed!

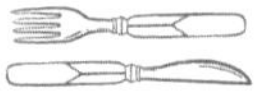

God will strengthen you with His own great power so that you will not give up when troubles come, but you will be patient. And you will joyfully give thanks to the Father who has made you able to have a share in all that He has prepared for His people in the kingdom of light.

COLOSSIANS 1:11–12 NCV

"I'm so stuffed! I'm too full to eat another bite," Sophia said as she pushed her plate away and started to get up from the table. Just then, her mom walked into the room with a plate of brownies, fresh out of the oven. "Well, maybe I have a little room left!" Sophia grinned.

Is it possible to be stuffed so full of joy, of God's goodness, of His amazing blessings that we just can't take anymore? But when another blessing comes, we would likely change our minds! Sometimes we can say to God by our choices or attitudes, *I'm stuffed, God. I've seen all I need to see of You in my life; I've been changed as much as I want to be changed; I've gone as far with You as I want to go.* Jesus said that if we hunger and thirst for righteousness, we will be filled. Paul prayed that we would be filled with the fullness of the Lord. How hungry are you for all the things God has for you? How strong is your desire to love Him more and see more of His work in your life?

No matter how far you go with the Lord, there is always more to experience. Don't settle for less! Wait at His table as long as it takes to be filled with Him.

Dear Lord,
I want more of You in my life:
more of Your love, Your presence,
Your joy! Thank You for filling me
up and then offering me even more.
Amen.

DISCUSSION PROMPT:

In what ways do you want to experience more of God? What can you do to make that happen?

The Most Important Thing

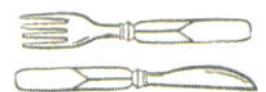

We will not hide these truths from our children; we will tell the next generation about the glorious deeds of the Lord, about His power and His mighty wonders.

PSALM 78:4, 6–7 NLT

Of all the lessons your parents taught you, what would you say is the most important? Younger children might say it's to look both ways before crossing the street. School-age kids might take their parents' advice on how to make and keep friends or how to work hard at school or in sports. Young adults might appreciate their parents' advice on finances or dating and marriage.

All those things are well and good, and God's plan was that parents remain in their children's lives to teach them the things they need to know to live successfully in our world. But none of those things could compare to the value of parents teaching their children how to trust in the Lord. Of course, trusting God isn't something that can be forced on a child; it is demonstrated day in and day out by parents and other influential grown-ups who trust God themselves, who show by example what it means to have a relationship with God and turn to Him for their needs.

When they do this, sharing the "glorious deeds of the Lord," they give their children far more than just good advice; they set a relationship with God as their foundation for life—the most important thing.

Dear Lord,
thank You for godly parents
who demonstrate by example
how to trust in You. Help us always
to lean on You in every situation
and pass our legacy of faith to
the next generation.
Amen.

DISCUSSION PROMPT:

What are some important lessons you learned from your own parents? What does it mean to trust God, and how are you learning to do so?

Who Knows You?

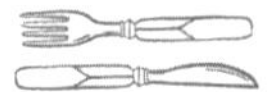

Before I shaped you in the womb,
I knew all about you.
Before you saw the light of day,
I had holy plans for you.

JEREMIAH 1:5 THE MESSAGE

On a trip to Washington, DC, Tyler was excited to visit the White House and see the president of the United States as he left the building and walked over to his motorcade. Near the front of the crowd, Tyler waved and called out the president's name, and to his surprise, the president turned and waved back. That is likely as close as Tyler will get to "knowing" the president; even though the president responded to him, he doesn't really know Tyler other than as someone in a crowd.

Your relationship with God is so much different. Even before you were born, God knew your name and had a wonderful life planned for you. He doesn't relate to you as a nameless person in the crowd; you are an individual, completely unique, and He knows you inside and out.

Let it comfort you today to remember that God knows your greatest fears, your deepest hurts, your hopes and your dreams.

And His love for you will never change! You don't have to hide anything from Him—you couldn't anyway!—because nothing you think, say, or do will alter how He feels about you. Who knows you? The God of the universe!

Dear Lord,
You know me! Even more than that, You love me as I am! I'm so grateful that You know me–inside and out–and that nothing will ever change Your great love for me.
Amen.

DISCUSSION PROMPT:

What famous person would you meet in real life if you could? What does it mean to you to know that God knows you by name?

The King Has Come Down

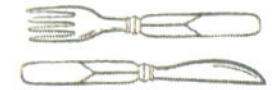

No one has ever gone up into the presence of God except the One who came down from that Presence, the Son of Man.

JOHN 3:13 THE MESSAGE

Throughout history, members of royalty have rarely come down from their high places of prestige and honor to actually mingle with commoners. If anything, they wave from the balconies of their palaces, but a king would never come out of the castle to play a round of golf with the locals, and the queen would likely never show up at the corner Starbucks to get her coffee. So how crazy is it that the King of kings—the Lord of the entire universe—has actually left His throne and entered our world, becoming one of us?

When this King came, though, He didn't come to simply hang out with the commoners, playing games or sipping lattes. He came to do what only He could do: make a way back to the Father for us. Not only that, but this King is the true King of hearts. Our hearts are what He wants from us. When we bow our knee to Him and invite Him into our lives, He will fill us with His presence and change us from the inside out.

Dear Jesus,

You left the riches and privileges of heaven, humbling Yourself to enter our world and become one of us. Thank You for opening the way to the Father. Be the King and the Lord of my life, now and always. Amen.

DISCUSSION PROMPT:

Have you ever met someone who was considered "royalty"? How different from a "commoner" did they seem? What does it mean to you that the King of the universe loves you?

Conversation Starters

*How are you most like your mother?
Your father?*

*What qualities do you
look for in a friend?*

Who has more fun: adults or kids?

*What's the scariest thing that has ever
happened to you?*

*What family rule would you
most like to change?*

*What fear would you
most like to conquer?*

God on Display

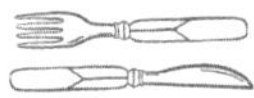

The LORD said to Moses, "Return to Pharaoh and make your demands again. I have made him and his officials stubborn so I can display My miraculous signs among them. I've also done it so you can tell your children and grandchildren about how I made a mockery of the Egyptians and about the signs I displayed among them—and so you will know that I am the LORD."

EXODUS 10:1–2 NLT

Lots of people seek to make their names famous. "Social influencer" is a career objective, as people strive to get the most likes or views on TikTok, YouTube, or other social media platforms.

When God wanted to tell the world about Himself, He took a different approach. Rather than setting up a website or trying to gain more followers on Twitter, He chose to use His dealings with His chosen people to show the world His character, power, and glory. When He brought the children of Israel out of slavery in Egypt and into the Promised Land, He did not destroy Egypt completely, but as He told Moses, His plan was "to show you my power and to spread my fame throughout the earth" (Exodus 9:16 NLT). And through the Exodus story, God was demonstrating the future redemption He had planned for all people.

Just as God displayed His power through the lives of His people thousands of years ago, He wants to show forth His glory through your life as well. He wants to put His love and mercy on display by working in your heart, your family, and your situation as you trust in Him.

Dear Lord,
may my life be a demonstration of Your power, glory, love, and grace to those around me. I trust You to do a mighty work in me.
Amen.

DISCUSSION PROMPT:

Do you follow any "influencers" on social media? If so, what is it about them that captures your attention? How can you share God's work in your life in a new and creative way?

Every Day of Your Life

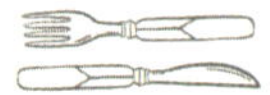

You saw me before I was born. Every day of my life was recorded in Your book. Every moment was laid out before a single day had passed.

PSALM 139:16 NLT

What is the most significant day of your life so far? The day you were born seems pretty important—enough to celebrate it every year! Maybe it's the day you graduated or got married or a child was born into your family. We all have sad days too. The day a loved one dies can be a life-changing day to many people. Maybe you were in an accident or received a devastating health diagnosis. No matter what happens to you in the course of a day, God already knew what was going to happen; nothing comes as a surprise to Him.

In Psalm 139, David thanks God that "every moment" of his life was planned before he was even born. He knew what David would do and who he would become, and even how long his life would last. When we are having a great day, it's easy to give thanks to God for planning that day for us. But on challenging days, sad days, difficult days to manage, it may be harder to believe that He is still in control. The good news is that He is.

We can be comforted by the fact that His plans for our lives are good, and that nothing that happens to us comes as a surprise to Him. No matter what you are facing this day, He is with you. He will see you through.

Dear Lord,
You have known every detail
of my life before I was ever born,
and I'm so grateful that nothing
that happens to me comes as a
surprise to You. Help me to trust
You not only in the good days,
but also in the bad, and remember
that Your plans for my life are
for my ultimate good.
Amen.

DISCUSSION PROMPT:

What do you think has been the best day of your life so far? The worst? How have you seen God's hand in either or both of those days?

He's Listening

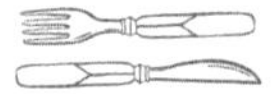

God says, "At just the right time, I heard you. On the day of salvation, I helped you." Indeed, the "right time" is now. Today is the day of salvation.

II CORINTHIANS 6:2 NLT

Have you ever tried to tell a friend some amazing news, but you could tell they weren't really paying attention? Or maybe you tried to tell a family member about your day, but all they did was nod and absentmindedly respond "Uh-huh." You knew the message didn't get through.

We might be tempted to think that God is like other people, who sometimes listen and sometimes don't. If He doesn't respond right away, we might wonder if He even heard us at all. The good news is that God is *not* like people—not at all. He is never too busy to listen to the prayers of His children, and He's never distracted or focused on something else when we come to Him with what's on our hearts. In fact, in those times when we pour out our true heart to Him, sharing our struggles, worries, fears, and needs, He draws near to us. He bends His ear to us to hear our heart. Be confident when you pray that He's listening, and that He cares.

Dear Lord,
even when it seems that
others aren't really listening, I know
You always are. You are a good
God who loves to hear the prayers
of Your children. Thank You for
listening to me today.
Amen.

DISCUSSION PROMPT:

Why do you think God listens so closely to us? What would He love to hear the most?

"Pick Me!"

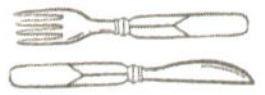

God chooses people according to His own purposes; He calls people, but not according to their good or bad works.

ROMANS 9:11–12 NLT

You can probably remember in elementary school when teams were chosen on the playground or when you knew the answer to the teacher's question and raised your hand to be called on. How badly did you want to be picked? All of us want to be "chosen"—asked to prom, picked for the cheerleading squad, promoted at work, elected to office. We try to make ourselves look good, rehearse what we will say, even change our appearance, all as an attempt to say, "Pick me! Pick me!"

No matter what human beings choose you for in this life, you can be confident that God has chosen you specifically, and He has a wonderful purpose for your life that only you can fulfill. His methods of choosing are far different from ours. He doesn't use human criteria, such as looks, wealth, or worldly prestige. "The Lord doesn't see things the way you see them. People judge by outward appearance, but the Lord looks at the heart" (I Samuel 16:7 NLT).

God looks at a heart that is turned toward Him and knows

He can use that person for His purposes on the earth. That is why Paul could write these words: "Remember, dear brothers and sisters, that few of you were wise in the world's eyes or powerful or wealthy when God called you. Instead, God chose things the world considers foolish in order to shame those who think they are wise. And He chose things that are powerless to shame those who are powerful" (I Corinthians 1:26–27 NLT). Don't worry about how much wealth, power, or influence you have. God can use you just the way you are. All He needs is your willing heart!

Dear Lord,
I want to be used by You. Pick me! Whatever You want me to do, my heart is willing to do. Thank You for choosing me and demonstrating Your purposes through my life.
Amen.

DISCUSSION PROMPT:

What criteria do you use when choosing someone to be a teammate? A study partner? A friend? Why are those characteristics important to you?

Here's the Proof

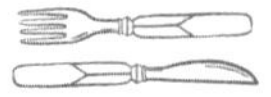

Now if we have died with Christ,
we believe that we will also live with him.

ROMANS 6:8 ESV

Have you ever had a friend who told you that they loved you but never actually did anything to show it? What if they claimed to be your friend to other people but never spent any time with you or even returned your calls? Could you really call that person your friend? Would you actually feel loved?

Thankfully, God is not like that. When He tells us He loves us, He backs it up with His actions. He sent Jesus to the earth to show us what His love is like. Jesus walked among us, sharing our hurts and sorrows. He touched and healed people, even raised them from the dead. And He went to the cross to open the way for us to live eternally with Him. What is the proof of God's love? Even before we loved Him in return, Jesus came to earth and died in our place.

Paul wrote this prayer to his friends: "May you have the power to understand, as all God's people should, how wide, how long, how high, and how deep His love is. May you experience the love of Christ, though it is too great to understand fully.

Then you will be made complete with all the fullness of life and power that comes from God" (Ephesians 3:18–19 NLT). God has proved His love for you! Let this amazing truth sink deep into your heart today.

Dear Lord,
You love me! I know this because of all You have done for me, but especially because You died on the cross in my place. Draw me into a deeper understanding of Your love each day as I spend time with You.
Amen.

DISCUSSION PROMPT:

When someone tells you they love you, what kinds of things would make you believe them? How has God shown His love for you in your life recently?

Making Himself at Home

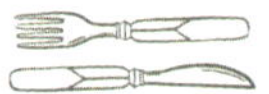

Christ will make His home in your hearts as you trust in Him. Your roots will grow down into God's love and keep you strong.

EPHESIANS 3:17 NLT

What makes a house a home? Most people would answer that it's the presence of the people you love, family members, even cherished pets. When you move to a new house, it can take some time to settle in and begin to feel at home, but as new memories are made and experiences are shared, what was once unfamiliar becomes a place of safety and belonging.

The Bible tells us that when we invite Him in, Jesus will come and make His home within our hearts. That means He's more than just a visitor who spends a few days seeing the sites and having a good time. He's not a houseguest that we need to pamper with fresh towels and sheets before He packs up His bags and heads out the door. No, He wants to move in with us and make Himself at home—right in the midst of our messy, beautiful, frustrating, loud, crazy families. Right in the middle of our relationships, struggles, heartaches, and joys. He wants to be *with us*. That's what the name Emmanuel means: "God with us." But He won't just barge through the door; we have to let Him in. He will make His home in our hearts as we put our trust in Him.

Dear Lord,
come into my heart,
come into my life,
and make Yourself
at home with me.
Amen.

DISCUSSION PROMPT:

How many places have you lived in your life? Which felt the most like home to you? How does it make you feel to think of Jesus "moving in": Hopeful? Apprehensive? Excited? Why?

Old Enough

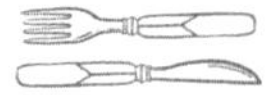

Don't let anyone treat you as if you are unimportant because you are young. Instead, be an example to the believers with your words, your actions, your love, your faith, and your pure life.

1 TIMOTHY 4:12 NCV

When we are young, it seems like it will take forever to grow up. We can't ride the cool roller coaster at the fair until we are four feet tall. We aren't big enough to swim in the deep end of the pool or ride a bike without training wheels. We have to wait to get our driver's licenses, graduate from high school, and on and on. But what we are never too young to do is use the talents and gifts God has put within us to be an example to other people and show what He is doing in our lives.

The prophet Jeremiah thought he was too young when God called him to share His message with other people. He likely was used to thinking of himself as "not old enough" in other areas of his life, but God made it clear what He wanted: "'O Sovereign Lord,' [Jeremiah] said, 'I can't speak for You! I'm too young!' The Lord replied, 'Don't say, "I'm too young," for you must go wherever I send you and say whatever I tell you'" (Jeremiah 1:6–7 NLT).

No matter how young you are—or how old—God has a plan for your life, and He needs you to fulfill your purpose. He wants a relationship with you and to show Himself strong in your life. Whatever your age, you're old enough to know Him, to love Him, and to follow Him. Listen for His voice speaking to you today.

Dear Lord,
starting today, whatever age
I am, I want to serve You all the
days of my life. Thank You for
unfolding Your wonderful purpose
for me as I follow You.
Amen.

DISCUSSION PROMPT:

What do you hope to do when you get older? What do you wish you had done when you were younger? How have you seen God working in the different times and stages of your life?

What's in Your Closet?

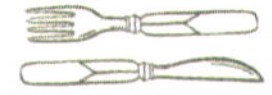

Don't be concerned about the outward beauty of fancy hairstyles, expensive jewelry, or beautiful clothes. You should clothe yourselves instead with the beauty that comes from within, the unfading beauty of a gentle and quiet spirit, which is so precious to God.

1 PETER 3:3–4 NLT

Clothes are an important part of people's lives. What we wear tells other people a lot about us: what we think is cool, what groups we identify with, how we approach life, and how much—or how little—we want other people to notice about us.

God knows how important our needs for clothing are. When Jesus reminded us of how our heavenly Father clothes the lilies of the field (Matthew 6:28–29), He told us not to worry so much about what we would wear. Far more than the clothes we wear on our bodies, God is concerned about how we clothe ourselves spiritually. When we put on mercy, humility, gentleness, kindness, and patience, we are far better dressed than many others, even if we don't have on the latest fashion trends. In Romans, Paul wrote that we should "clothe [ourselves] with the presence of the Lord Jesus Christ" (13:14 NLT). Imagine how our lives would be different if we "wore" Jesus' presence all day, responding to each situation with His grace and love?

Dear Lord,
it's easy to get caught up in concerns about my outward appearance. Help me to remember that what matters to You is what is on the inside. I want to clothe myself with Your presence, bringing You with me through my day, sharing Your love, joy, and peace with everyone I meet.
Amen.

DISCUSSION PROMPT:

What is your favorite item of clothing? What makes it your favorite? How can you remind yourself each morning to clothe yourself with God's presence, just as you put on your outward clothes?

A Teachable Heart

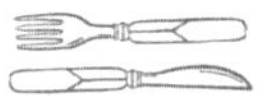

O God, you have taught me from my earliest childhood, and I constantly tell others about the wonderful things You do.

PSALM 71:17 NLT

Are you someone who likes to learn? Are you a person who can be taught? Do you know the difference between the two?

People who can be taught are willing to set their pride aside and admit they don't know everything there is to know. They don't resent it when someone shows them something they didn't know or a better way to do something. And they aren't satisfied with what they already know—they are hungry to learn more!

The best teacher we could ever have is the Holy Spirit. In order to learn from Him, you must have a spirit of humility and be willing to listen to Him when He speaks to you. And He will! The Bible tells us that He teaches us, even in the earliest years of our childhood. When we don't know which way to go or what to do in a difficult situation, He will guide our steps. He will lead us into greater understanding of Himself and a deeper relationship with our heavenly Father.

Holy Spirit,
You are the greatest Teacher I could ever have. I want to learn everything You want to teach me. Help me maintain a teachable heart and listen for Your voice as You lead and guide me all of my days. Amen.

DISCUSSION PROMPT:

What new talent or skill would you like to learn? How would a spirit of humility help you to learn this skill? What has the Holy Spirit taught you recently?

Group Activity

NATURE WALK

Take a family walk around the neighborhood or through a city park. Collect leaves for a leaf collection; count how many animals you see; spend time thanking God for His marvelous creation!

Dear Friend,

This book was prayerfully crafted with you, the reader, in mind. Every word, every sentence, every page was thoughtfully written, designed, and packaged to encourage you—right where you are this very moment. At DaySpring, our vision is to see every person experience the life-changing message of God's love. So, as we worked through rough drafts, design changes, edits, and details, we prayed for you to deeply experience His unfailing love, indescribable peace, and pure joy. It is our sincere hope that through these Truth-filled pages your heart will be blessed, knowing that God cares about you—your desires and disappointments, your challenges and dreams.

He knows. He cares. He loves you unconditionally.

BLESSINGS!

THE DAYSPRING BOOK TEAM